ADVANCE PRAISE FOR

A Hundred Thousand Orphans

"This vivid and absorbing book is a work of ethical depth—a triumph of scholarship, thought and empathy. Peter H. Wolff, who has dedicated his illustrious professional life to the study of how children grow and develop, has now written a spellbinding account of his work with the abandoned victims of the Eritrean-Ethiopian war, the Eritrean orphans. While this is a provocative and fascinating book on the forces of idealism and rebellion that shaped the war, his first-hand account does nothing less than revolutionize our notions about how children can recover from trauma and grow up to become self-reliant, productive adults. Moreover, he brings the art of the storyteller through this narrative—big themes mingle with personal tragedy, which makes it not only intellectually challenging and emotionally exhilarating but compulsively readable. His ability to draw out arresting examples and comparisons and to combine psychological, political, demographic, environmental and cultural analysis is impressive, so that no one reading this volume can fail to learn a great deal. This vivid and riveting book is a celebration of the human imagination and the human heart."

—Kevin Nugent, Founder and Director of the Brazelton Institute, Division of Developmental Medicine, Boston Children's Hospital; Professor Emeritus, University of Massachusetts; Lecturer, Harvard Medical School

"This is a thoroughly absorbing personal memoir by a wise and thoughtful psychiatrist who had the unique experience of observing the effects of war on a nation's children. Peter Wolff provides an insightful and vivid account of the effect of early traumatic experience on childhood development and the strength of the Eritrean people. This description of the events in Eritrea from 1985 to 2015 is full of wisdom, insight, compassion, and humility by a truly outstanding observer."

— George F. Michel, Ph.D., Emeritus Professor of Psychology, University of North Carolina Greensboro

"*A Hundred Thousand Orphans* provides a fascinating inside look at the impact a creative, empowering approach to education can have on severely traumatized children, most of whom were orphaned or abandoned during Eritrea's long war for independence from Ethiopia. This makes the speed with which the postwar regime squandered these breakthroughs in favor of tight social controls and traditional rote learning and memorization all the more disheartening. Nevertheless, Wolff's rigorous documentation of the successful initial experiment offers valuable lessons for anyone dealing with the effects of trauma on children and the healing power of affection and mutual respect, together with a stark warning against taking such achievements for granted. Wolff also argues that the vision behind this pioneering experiment will live on through the survivors to see another day in the sun. I, for one, was convinced."

— Dan Connell, Author of *Against All Odds* (1997), *Conversations with Eritrean Political Prisoners* (2005), and *Historical Dictionary of Eritrea* (2019)

"I am writing this letter to endorse the works of Peter Wolff. To write a letter of recommendation of an accomplished author, scientist and educator like Peter Wolff is not an easy task. If, nevertheless, he has honored me by the invitation to write this letter, and if I gladly accepted, it is because this letter of support offers an occasion that permits clarifying the nature of a common experience we shared during the darkest moment of Eritrean history. I met the author decades ago in the Sahel, the most inaccessible northern region of Eritrea, where the devastation of the liberation war of attrition that lingered for a quarter of a century combined with biblical drought devastated the population. The Eritrean liberation fighters built underground hospitals and clinics and provided basic health services to the nomadic pastoralists, displaced populations and orphanages.

In these testing hours a professor from Boston (Harvard) unexpectedly appeared in the night at Orotta, the central hospital of the liberation front, after crisscrossing the eastern desert of Sudan and climbing the hills of Sahel, riding on the cargo trucks by night. Although I was intrigued, his mere appearance was a source of hope to all of us, especially at that particular time of loneliness and isolation when solidarity is more valued than any material help. I asked him, 'You came all the way from Harvard to this wretched part of the planet. Why?' He simply said, 'To help' and 'help' he did.

In his humble but ambitious book, Peter Wolff endeavors to reflect on and ascertain his unique study among the displaced Eritrean orphans living in the rugged mountains in underground bunkers, makeshift tents and caves, distant from civilization but safe from military incursion, deep in the hills of Sahel, a province that was under the control of the Eritreans. The orphans lived communally until adulthood. Food was scarce, but under an acacia tree they gathered in groups of ten around a plate—a flat slab of stone—where sorghum bread with sparse lentils was served. No meat, vegetables, or fruits. It was a miserable life, to say the least. Those who took care of the orphans were young men and women liberation fighters who had neither the knowledge nor the desire to work with children because they joined the front to fight, not to nurture orphans. The arrival of a foreign expert from afar transformed the mood of the workers and in good spirit they listened and absorbed all the advice and instruction given by Dr. Wolff and applied it religiously. His advice drastically transformed the facilities' structure, staffing pattern, and outcome of the orphanages.

The reader is taken on a journey through hardships and challenges, elaborating first-hand the saga of a study that spans two decades. This journey involves liberation fighters, officials of the state of Eritrea, and orphans at various stages of their lives. The tone of the book reflects a learned appreciation of the dedicated people and committed leaders, with a humble academic base but unbeatable will combined with scientific input from one of the best minds, a product of the most prestigious institution, who lived, experienced first-hand, and saw it all.

Peter Wolff's investigation and conclusions are based on detailed examination of the records of the orphans, systematic surveys and in-depth analyses of his meticulous recording, including personal interviews of orphans, whom he followed from childhood to adulthood. In his study he finds compelling evidence that is contrary to the accepted school of thought and proposes recommendations that are not conventional. He negates the rigidly assured adverse impact on children institutionalized in orphanages for a long time—especially those who are victims of conflict in poor and underdeveloped societies—and concludes that under a stimulating environment and appropriate care they are equal if not better in terms of social, cognitive and physical development when compared to parented children.

This book is an excellent resource for students and educators, and above all it is a tribute to those who made it possible under circumstances meshed with war, hunger, displacement and desperation. It is also a testimony to the populations in poor countries that orphans are not doomed, unfortunate victims but instead, with minimal material comforts and abundant love and support, they can turn into citizens equal if not better than those who grow up with their families. The author demonstrates the detailed progression of a long-term follow-up that spans over a generation, shedding light on the good will and compassion of workers who created unexpected outcomes in a place far in Africa, ridden with impossibilities.

The author's writing is eloquent and understandable at all levels. It is a well-documented book with conclusions that could be arrived at by others, but above all, it is a treasure trove of science and humanity with relevance to society at large today and a long time into the future."

— Assefaw Tekeste Ghebrekidan MD, Dr PH, Public Health Program, Professor, College of Education and Health Sciences, Touro University California

A Hundred Thousand Orphans

Studies in Criticality

Shirley R. Steinberg
General Editor

Vol. 538

Peter H. Wolff

A Hundred Thousand Orphans

My Experience with the Children of the Eritrean War

PETER LANG
Lausanne • Berlin • Bruxelles • Chennai • New York • Oxford

Library of Congress Cataloging-in-Publication Control Number: 2022050518

Bibliographic information published by the **Deutsche Nationalbibliothek**.
The German National Library lists this publication in the German
National Bibliography; detailed bibliographic data is available
on the Internet at http://dnb.d-nb.de.

Cover design by Peter Lang Group AG

ISSN 1058-1634
ISBN 978-1-63667-012-6 (hardback)
ISBN 978-1-4331-9984-4 (paperback)
ISBN 978-1-4331-9982-0 (ebook pdf)
ISBN 978-1-4331-9983-7 (epub)
DOI 10.3726/b20376

© 2023 Peter Lang Group AG, Lausanne
Published by Peter Lang Publishing Inc., New York, USA
info@peterlang.com - www.peterlang.com

All rights reserved.
All parts of this publication are protected by copyright.
Any utilization outside the strict limits of the copyright law, without the permission of the
publisher, is forbidden and liable to prosecution.
This applies in particular to reproductions, translations, microfilming, and storage and
processing in electronic retrieval systems.

This publication has been peer reviewed.

To the children of Eritrea

TABLE OF CONTENTS

List of Figures		xi
Preface		xiii
Acknowledgments		xvii
Introduction		1
Part I	**Eritrea at War**	5
Chapter 1	The Road to the Base Camps	7
Chapter 2	A Brief Overview of Modern Eritrea	17
Chapter 3	The Base Camps	25
Chapter 4	The Human Factor	35

Chapter 5	Departures	41
Chapter 6	Solomuna	45
Chapter 7	Solomuna Revisited	57
Chapter 8	Centers for Mothers and Infants	61
Chapter 9	The Zero School	65
Chapter 10	Cassandra's List	79
Chapter 11	Peace at Last	87
Part II	**One Hundred Thousand Orphans**	93
Chapter 12	Meeting the Challenge	95
Chapter 13	Orphanages	99
Chapter 14	Reunification	111
Chapter 15	Group Homes	121
Chapter 16	Education after Liberation	131
Chapter 17	Community Child-Care Centers	137
Part III	**A Dubious Liberation**	151
Chapter 18	A New Government	153
Chapter 19	Another War	157
Chapter 20	The Peacetime Economy and Its Ramifications	161

Part IV	**The Legacy of the Zero School**	165
Chapter 21	The Orphans Revisited	167
Chapter 22	Looking Forward	173
	Bibliography	179
	Additional Resources	183
	Biographical Data	189

LIST OF FIGURES

Figure 1.	Children in the Asmara orphanage taking a break from activities.	140
Figure 2.	Teacher playing with the children in the orphanage playground.	140
Figure 3.	Two of the combatants working in the underground electronics workshop.	141
Figure 4.	Students planting vegetables at the Zero School – an example of "Theory and Praxis" agriculture.	141
Figure 5.	Caregiver with children at breakfast. (Asmara Orphanage)	142
Figure 6.	Lunchtime in the group home.	142
Figure 7.	Several of the children sleeping in an underground cave, where they're protected from the bombing raids.	143
Figure 8.	Students in class at the Zero School.	144
Figure 9.	The group home mascot.	145
Figure 10.	Friends posing for the camera. (Asmara Orphanage)	146
Figure 11.	Asmara Orphanage.	146
Figure 12.	The house mother and Tarik after he returned to his group home.	147
Figure 13.	Air raid.	147

Figure 14.	Children heading off for their bath.	148
Figure 15.	Students attending class in the Zero School.	148
Figure 16.	Movie night under the stars.	149
Figure 17.	A snapshot of the underground pharmacy where the most essential pharmaceuticals were produced.	149
Figure 18.	Producing pharmaceuticals in the underground pharmacy.	150

PREFACE

In its 2005 annual report on *The State of the World's Children*, the United Nations Children's Fund estimated that armed conflict, drought, famine, and other unnatural disasters have deprived more than 60 million children of their families, their homes, and, ultimately, their identity.[1] What happens to these children? What steps can be taken while they are still children that will give them a fair chance for a livable life? And what can their stories teach us about the effects of early experience on childhood development? These are global questions that have no global answers. Yet they must be asked and, whenever possible, be addressed at a local level.

Conventional wisdom holds that abuse, human cruelty, or trauma of some sort early in life will have serious negative outcomes. It may be, however, that the ability of children to rebound from the effects of early traumatic experience has much to do with the *cause* of that trauma: that is, whether it was due to maltreatment by other human beings (physical abuse, sexual abuse, deliberate injury of any sort) or to the consequences of man's inhumanity to man (war, starvation, extreme poverty, etc.). This book tells the story of Eritrean orphans who spent their most vulnerable years of childhood under tremendous adversity but grew up to become self-reliant, productive adults with the courage to resist the authority of those who threatened their basic human rights and universal democratic freedoms. From their story, one can conclude that when the social (and ideological) conditions are right, vulnerable children can grow up to become remarkably healthy and ethically sound adults.

Eritrea is a small, poor country on the volatile Horn of Africa, a country whose people fought a thirty-year war for freedom and independence from Ethiopia. During that time, it educated a whole generation of children and laid the foundations for an open, democratic society. To get some idea of the conditions that made Eritrea's foray into social democracy possible, I visited the base camps of the Eritrean People's Liberation Front (EPLF) in 1985. What I discovered there was so extraordinary that I returned again and again thereafter.

I quickly learned that, if I wanted to understand what had made Eritrea's social revolution even possible, I would have to learn many things about the country's history, its cultural traditions, its child-rearing practices, its values, and its peculiar brand of Marxism. However, much of what I wanted to learn about its children I would probably not find in newspaper articles, pamphlets, or any of the excellent books that have been written about modern Eritrea. Instead, I would have to learn for myself by observing the children in their natural environment both in times of war and of peace and, wherever appropriate, by interacting with them and their caregivers.

Accordingly, after a brief description of the country's geography, people, culture, and struggle for independence, Part I of this book establishes the wartime landscape and traumatic context in which the thousands of orphans and other lost children of Eritrea found themselves. Here I set the stage by recounting my early experiences visiting the base camps and medical facilities; interacting with the combatants, the doctors, and the children; and learning about the values by which they all lived. Within that framework, I also describe how the human factor—the courage, personal commitment, and self-discipline of the combatants—made this extraordinary experiment in nation building possible; how the EPLF rehabilitated and educated all the children in their care; and how, as part of this effort, the combatants integrated the best practices of the traditional village community with the goal of universal literacy and the progressive values of their social revolution.

Part II reviews the various programs and institutions that the postwar government used to reintegrate its hundred thousand orphans into their communities. From my personal experiences visiting the orphanages, reunified families, and small group homes, I was able to see firsthand how the children who had survived the trauma of war were, under the aegis of the EPLF, continuing to mature and flourish.

Part III looks at what happened to Eritrea's revolution once the external enemy had been defeated, only to be replaced by an internal dictatorship, and the values that had fueled the thirty-year struggle for independence were deemed no longer essential for the country's survival as a sovereign state.

Finally, Part IV looks at how efforts to expand and fine-tune the progressive education practiced in the base camps fared after the fighting stopped. And returning to the original premise about the ability of children to survive and thrive after a childhood of extreme adversity and loss, I compare the development of Eritrea's orphans (who had internalized and practiced the values of the EPLF) with the development of those children whose lives were not dramatically disrupted by the war, who had not lost their families or their homes, and who had been schooled in accordance with the more traditional educational practices that flourished elsewhere. And with an eye toward the future, I speculate about how the children in whom those EPLF values were inculcated may be able not only to flourish in the face of the radical antidemocratic transformation of Eritrea's postwar government, but also to oppose that government, reunite their country, and restore the dream of a truly liberated, just, and democratic society.

Note

1 United Nations Children's Fund (UNICEF), *The State of the World's Orphans 2005: Childhood under Threat* (New York: UNICEF, 2004). https://www.unicef.org/sowc/archive/ENGLISH/The%20State%20of%20the%20World%27s%20Children%202005.pdf

ACKNOWLEDGMENTS

My thanks are due to Andemariam Gebremichael (whom you will meet in the following pages as Andu); to Dr. Assefaw Tekeste, the bravest man I have ever met; and to Jane Cotnoir, my editor, without whom this story would never have been fit for publication.

INTRODUCTION

Sometime in the early 1980s, three fierce-looking young men with impressive Afro haircuts knocked on my office door at Boston Children's Hospital and introduced themselves as Eritreans. I didn't know what to make of that introduction, because I didn't have the slightest idea what or where Eritrea was. Judging by their hairstyle, their accent, and their demeanor, I assumed that they must be from one of the many postcolonial countries springing up all over West and East Africa. To orient me, their spokesman, Andemariam Gebremichael, or Andu, unrolled a large wall map of Africa, which he had brought with him, and pointed to a curiously shaped piece of real estate on the Red Sea coast, which he identified as his homeland, Eritrea. When I asked why the area to which he pointed was identified on the map as a province of Ethiopia, he launched into a long, fascinating account of Eritrea's thirty-year war of liberation from Ethiopia, describing how the people of Eritrea were combating the far superior Ethiopian juggernaut while, at the same time, trying to transform their backward peasant society into a literate and progressive modern society based on democratic principles of equality and social justice.

Even if only half of what Andu told me about the Eritrean struggle was accurate, it should have commanded the attention and profound respect of political scientists, sociologists, and the leaders of other postcolonial countries fighting for their freedom and independence.

But I still didn't understand why he was telling me about all these remarkable achievements in a country somewhere in East Africa. To explain, Andu finally reminded me that, more than ten years ago, I had belonged to a small group of American doctors, nurses, and other citizens who were outraged over America's wars in Vietnam, Cambodia, and Laos. Our organization worked to raise funds from like-minded American citizens for urgently needed medications and medical equipment. Because I happened to be in Hanoi on the night when the U.S. Air Force bombed the Bach Mai Hospital in the center of the city, I was able to document the bombardment on film, proving that the report of the bombing was not a Vietnamese propaganda stunt. As the film showed, the beds in the pediatric wing of the hospital were filled with terribly wounded children. With such documentation at our disposal, we were able to raise large amounts of private and public donations in the United States to buy robust and reliable but inexpensive medical equipment from various European countries and Japan.

Now, ten years later, the Eritrean community in Boston wanted to do something along the same lines for the large underground central hospital in the EPLF base camps, and they needed advice on how to proceed without getting into difficulties with American authorities for "trading with the enemy." (Even though the United States was not at war with the EPLF, it was sending huge consignments of military hardware to Ethiopia. The Soviets, however, were the main supporters of the new Ethiopian military junta, a quasi-pseudo-Marxist regime.) Once I was convinced that these three young men were neither terrorists nor CIA provocateurs, I put them in touch with the person in our group who could conduct the delicate negotiations for sending medical equipment to a communist country.

I thought that that would be the end of the matter, but it wasn't. Over a year later, Andu came back, this time with an entirely different proposal. He had been instructed by his friends in the field to ask me whether I would consider visiting the base camps of the EPLF, so that I could report to the American public what I had seen and experienced in Eritrea.

When he first approached me with that proposition, I thought that patriotic fervor (fever?) must have clouded his mind. Evacuating napalm-burned children from South Vietnam for treatment in the United States, and later traveling to North Vietnam to help with the repair and reconstruction of the Bach Mai Hospital, had made good sense at the time. Not only would it help to rescue some war-injured children, but it would also make the American public painfully aware that the United States was waging a criminal war against the people of Vietnam, terrorizing them with napalm, cluster bombs, Agent Orange, white phosphorus, and five-thousand-pound "daisy-cutter" bombs—all in the name of freedom and democracy.

On the other hand, trekking twelve thousand miles to one of the most inaccessible corners of East Africa to tell Americans about the plight of the Eritrean people would almost certainly prove to be fruitless. Other than professional revolution watchers, almost no one in the United States had ever heard of Eritrea, and those who had, probably dismissed it as a desert wasteland, a corner of the world where tribesmen in loin clothes and sandals were attacking tanks with wooden spears. What, then, could I possibly accomplish by visiting the base camps of the Eritrean independence movement? So, sadly, I turned down Andu's proposition.

But the more I read about the recent history of Eritrea, the more I began to think that I had been too hasty in rejecting Andu's invitation. If Eritrea were really such a hopeless wasteland, why had so many journalists, historians, economists, political scientists, architects, and even paleontologists and archeologists written about it in such glowing terms, recounting its centuries-long history, the EPLF's revolutionary fighting spirit and brilliant military strategies, its perseverance against all odds, and its forward-looking plans for transforming a backward rural society into a modern nation-state? Why, for that matter, had Secretary of State Warren Christopher referred to Eritrea's struggle for independence as "a beacon of hope astride the Horn of Africa"?[1]

Perhaps there was something about this war that went far beyond armed conflict and that fundamentally distinguished Eritrea and its people from the many other newly emerging sovereign states in Africa.

But what I found most compelling about the invitation was that it might afford me some insight into the enduring developmental questions about the reversibility of severe traumatic experiences in early childhood and into the measures that could be taken to protect children from the ravages of war. So, after weighing the risks and benefits of Andu's invitation and discussing them with my family, I eventually agreed to go and see for myself how Eritrea's children were not only surviving but, in many respects, thriving in very difficult times and under impossible circumstances.

Note

1 Secretary of State Warren Christopher, "The United States and Africa: A New Relationship," address before the 23rd African-American Institute Conference, Reston, Va., May 21, 1993, http://dosfan.lib.uic.edu/ERC/briefing/dossec/1993/9305/930521dossec.html

Part I
Eritrea at War

· 1 ·

THE ROAD TO THE BASE CAMPS

Once I had accepted Andu's invitation, he briefed me on what I should expect in the EPLF base camps and how I should prepare myself for the journey. Foreigners who planned to visit the liberated areas of Eritrea in 1985 usually flew from Europe to Khartoum, where they received travel papers from the Sudanese embassy. These papers permitted me to travel to almost every place of interest in Sudan, but strictly forbade me to cross the border into territory already under EPLF control. The Sudanese authorities knew perfectly well that European or North American visitors who gave the refugee camps in Sudan as their destination were actually on their way to Eritrea, but, as long as no one talked about these territorial ambiguities, the government in Khartoum didn't care.

Malaria was the only disease that was endemic to the region of Eritrea where I would travel. Nevertheless, the Medical Department of the EPLF recommended prophylactic antimalarial drugs and a hefty dose of immune globulin. A sleeping bag and a working flashlight were essential; in many parts of Eritrea, there was no electricity and the only place to sleep was on the ground, competing for space with scorpions and snakes. Andu also recommended light, airy clothing in subdued colors so that the roving Ethiopian MIG fighter jets couldn't spot me. He assured me that no foreign visitors had been killed or injured in the liberated zones during the past five years, but he neglected to mention what had happened before then.

Port Sudan, in the northern corner of Sudan, was the staging area for all traffic going in and out of the base camps. Nura Muhammed, the local representative for the EPLF stationed in Khartoum, made sure that all the precious cargo on its way to the base camps had arrived safely in Port Sudan before our crossing of the border during the night. In her calm, unflappable way, Nura prepared me for the journey and recommended that I would find traveling by plane much more comfortable and also much safer than traveling by land. As it happened, the regular pilots for Sudan Air had been on strike for several weeks, but a Sudan Air official eventually found two Iraqi pilots who were willing to fly to Port Sudan, and we were on our way. As we took off, my parting image of the Sudan airport was of a half-dozen emaciated adolescent Dinka girls from Southern Sudan who had escaped the Arabic slave traders and now sold their bodies for a few pennies so they could feed their starving babies.

Before leaving Khartoum, I had been instructed to be on the lookout for a large, bright blue, three-story house on the outskirts of Port Sudan. The EPLF was renting this building, which it had converted into a hospital for severely injured combatants. The nurse in charge of the hospital had been alerted that an American doctor was on his way. She was probably expecting a trauma surgeon and might well have wondered what she was supposed to do with a psychiatrist. But she immediately took me in tow when I arrived and, after the obligatory cup of sweet tea, invited me to join her on her daily clinical rounds.

Many of the patients in this auxiliary hospital were combat casualties who had been evacuated from the front lines and brought to Port Sudan because the treatment they needed was not available at the front. Most were either paraplegics or double and triple amputees. Since the EPLF had almost no ambulances, the severely injured combatants had to be transported on the flatbeds of large trucks, which the doctors filled with a thick layer of sand to absorb some of the worst shocks of the twenty-four-hour journey from the field. There were also a few quadriplegic patients; having miraculously survived the evacuation from the front lines, they were now waiting to die in a foreign land.

The clinic staff consisted of several experienced surgical nurses who had themselves been combat casualties but were now functioning perfectly well, several barefoot doctors who had been trained in the field, a volunteer physiotherapist from the Netherlands, and an Eritrean combatant who had lost one leg in the front lines and was now in charge of a crew that manufactured prosthetic arms and legs in the adjacent brace shop.

Dr. Afeworki Abraham, the only neurosurgeon in the EPLF, was often needed in the field because, under local combat conditions, crippling head and spine injuries were all too common. Trained in Israel, he had worked as a neurosurgeon in the Ethiopian army, but when he had seen an opportunity to defect, he did, and in 1975 he joined the Medical Department of the EPLF. Whenever the Central Hospital in Orotta could spare him, he came to Port Sudan to monitor the status of the paraplegic patients and perform basic palliative surgery to relieve their unbearable muscle spasms.

On the ground floor of the clinic, some of the paraplegic patients were desperately pressing on their bellies to urinate while others were catheterizing themselves. The only drugs available at the clinic that might have controlled their violent spasms were so weak that they had to be given in doses that reduced the patients to zombies. Most of the patients therefore preferred to stay awake even if that meant having to tolerate egregious pain; a few quadriplegic patients were now playing cutthroat poker and cracking macabre jokes about their life expectancy.

The head nurse then invited me to join her for rounds on the second floor, where, I suspected, the most serious cases were kept. But I asked to be excused: I couldn't take any more. Maybe it was culture shock. Maybe it was the unbearable heat. Maybe it was looking into the faces of these young, terribly mangled boys and seeing death in their eyes. Maybe it was simply the foul stench of sweat, stale urine, and blood. But I had to get out into the open air so that I wouldn't break down and embarrass these brave people who couldn't afford the luxury of pity. Sensing my discomfort, the head nurse took me by the hand to a shady place outside the clinic, gave me some water, patted me on the back, and reassured me that it would be all right. But what would ever be all right again? Would these young men even live long enough to celebrate the independence for which they had sacrificed themselves?

The patients at the clinic—especially the paraplegic ones, mobilized in their rickety wheelchairs of World War I vintage—had formed a closely knit self-help community, which must have been a powerful source of strength for them. Ambulatory casualties limping on crutches helped others get out of bed or reinsert their Foley catheters. Some of the paraplegic patients were completing their high school education, which they had interrupted to join the EPLF; now they were concentrating on computer programming so they could get good jobs and perhaps even be able to live independently. Not once did I hear any of the paralyzed combatants doubt that the EPLF would ultimately prevail, even if they wouldn't live long enough to see it. Out on the sand flats, a few lonely paraplegic patients sat in their wheelchairs and stared out across to the Red Sea, probably thinking of the home they might never see again; others played wheelchair volleyball.

Twice a day, like clockwork, all ambulatory patients, nurses, and barefoot doctors who could be spared from clinical duties stopped whatever they were doing to huddle around large Japanese shortwave radios that had been liberated from the Ethiopian military storage buildings; combatants who were bed-ridden had their own radios. For the next hour they all sat with their ears glued to the radios. First on the unchanging daily menu was the clandestine Eritrean radio station "The Voice of the Masses," which summarized the news from an EPLF perspective and was broadcast in Tigre, Tigrinya, and Arabic. Next came "The Voice of Ethiopia," "The Voice of America," and "The Voice of Moscow," all three of which were broadcast in English and Amharic. Most of these broadcasts were so obviously filled with lies that they became the radio comedy hour for the wounded combatants.

But then came the familiar BBC musical jingle announcing that the daily "BBC Focus on Africa" was about to begin. The atmosphere of the clinic changed dramatically. Many of the wounded combatants had joined the EPLF when they were barely eighteen and had probably never gone to school, but, from the few words in their discussion that sounded familiar, I was impressed by how much better informed they were about world affairs than many U.S. college graduates.

On the morning of our third day at the clinic, Negussie, who was in charge of all transports from Port Sudan into the EPLF base camps, told us to gather our gear, as we would probably be leaving for Eritrea that evening. A slender man with a sad, abstracted face and a withered hand, Negussie once again reminded us that the road we would travel was the lifeline of the entire independence movement and therefore had to be protected at all costs. As foreign visitors who were about to cross the border, we should therefore keep our mouths shut and not interfere with the driver's delicate negotiations.

Departures to the field were always scheduled for the late afternoon so that travelers could ride during the night, eat and rest during the next day, and reach Eritrea at or just after sunset—in other words, after the Ethiopian MIGs had returned to home base. While we were waiting for our transport, the first contingent of twelve to fifteen Swedish, Italian, German, Dutch, Russian, and American trailer trucks—a truly international convoy—started the twenty-four-hour journey to the base camps. The trucks were loaded with everything imaginable, from large sacks of wheat and other foodstuffs to farm machinery and various kinds of military hardware. On top of all that were old men, women, and even young children who were hitching a ride home to the camps.

As guests of the EPLF, we had the luxury of traveling by Toyota Land Cruiser, which was much lighter than the powerful Land Rover that could more easily get stuck in the sand river. In all, there were five of us. I sat with the driver and a journalist in front. A mattress and a cot had been arranged on the back seat for a young female fighter who was recovering from a major operation that had been performed in Khartoum. A barefoot doctor sat with her for the entire journey, monitoring her intravenous fluids and, as long as his supply lasted, giving her morphine whenever she screamed in pain.

Our first stop on the way to the base camps was in Suakin, an ancient Turkish trading center on the Red Sea that had disintegrated shortly after the collapse of the Ottoman Empire and now, after many decades of neglect, had become a stopover for traders and tourists. Close by, the EPLF had built a huge open-air garage and fuel depot, which must have covered at least twenty acres. Before taking the treacherous roads to the base camps, all trucks and cars had to be carefully checked by the EPLF mechanics to make sure that they wouldn't break down on the way. Next to the garage, the EPLF had also built an auxiliary clinic where paraplegic ex-combatants who no longer needed constant medical attention could receive their daily hydrotherapy by being dipped into the soothing warm water of the Red Sea, which was thought to have great healing powers.

While we were waiting for the huge trailer trucks to pass inspection, I poked around in the Turkish ruins and came across a large, fenced-in area where there was a lot of hammering and sawing. Inside, six Eritrean carpenters and shipfitters were busily building wooden fishing dhows. As soon as they saw me watching them, they frantically waved their arms and shouted something I didn't understand, but they were clearly not about to invite me for a cup of tea. When I later asked our driver about the commotion, he laughed and explained that the men were building boats for the clandestine Eritrean navy. These wooden dhows, which could slip easily under the radar screen of the Soviet destroyer that constantly patrolled the Red Sea to prevent the EPLF from opening another supply route, would in time become the first ships of the EPLF navy and would play a critical role during the final battle for Massawa, the largest Eritrean harbor.

Once the EPLF had inspected and approved the convoy and we were under way again, the asphalt road abruptly stopped, replaced by a bewildering pattern of constantly changing sand ruts. Like all the EPLF drivers with whom I would travel this road in the future, our driver seemed to have a special instinct that told him exactly which of the tracks were safe and which were sand traps.

For long-forgotten reasons, a British-Chinese consortium had once built a paved road and a telephone line that linked Port Sudan with an important trading center in Tokar on the northern tip of Sudan. Our only guarantee that we were still on the road and not simply floundering in the dunes was an endless row of teetering telephone poles adorned with limp telephone wires flapping in the wind. And even these relics were slowly disappearing as the nomads cannibalized the wood for their cooking fires. Except for an occasional glimpse of the Red Sea on our left shimmering in the sunset, the desert now stretched endlessly in all directions.

The moment the sun disappeared behind the Sudanese foothills, wave after wave of jackrabbits and field mice, hypnotized by our headlights, crossed the road at just the wrong time, committing a kind of mass suicide. Far in the distance I could see the campfires of the nomads who had settled down in the dunes for the night and let their camels graze untethered, protected from thieves by vicious dogs.

As the dunes got higher and the ruts deeper, our patient in the back shrieked in agony and begged the barefoot doctor for morphine, but his supply had run out. Suddenly, there was a loud crack from somewhere deep inside the belly of the Land Cruiser, and the motor came to a dead stop. After inspecting the car's drivetrain, the driver casually shrugged his shoulders and, in his same calm tone, announced that the axle was broken. I was convinced that we were hopelessly stuck in the Sudanese desert and would have to continue on foot, but the driver grinned, and with a cheerful "not to worry," he set off on foot into the black night.

In less than an hour he was back, leading a monstrous Soviet truck that was bigger than any of the Soviet tanks I had seen in documentary films and had all the characteristics of a prehistoric monster. After a brief consultation, the driver of the truck hooked our car to the behemoth and pulled it like a toy to a large, fenced-in compound, which two EPLF combatants were guarding with their Kalashnikovs. When they turned on the klieg lights, the compound turned out to be another enormous garage in the middle of the desert. One corner was filled with a bewildering collection of American, English, Russian,

Japanese, Swedish, Italian, and Dutch trucks, bulldozers, and cars that had been either "liberated" from the Ethiopian army or donated by progressive European nongovernmental organizations (NGOs). Another corner was filled with mountains of spare parts, cannibalized trucks, pieces of bulldozers, and nearly all the technical equipment that one would expect to find in any large Western garage or machine shop.

The EPLF had built this garage in Sudan at the critical halfway point between Port Sudan and the base camps to ensure that neither mechanical failures, nor broken axles, nor flat tires, nor empty fuel tanks would ever disrupt this vital lifeline of the independence movement. The local inhabitants and Sudanese police knew exactly what the purpose of this garage was, but no one ever complained to the authorities because they knew that the expert mechanics would always be willing to help with repairs to the Sudanese buses when they broke down. In less than an hour, the mechanics had replaced the broken axle, the barefoot doctor had negotiated a few ampules of morphine for our patient, and we were again on our way.

Our next scheduled stop was Coro Baraka, a rest area that was still inside Sudan but was managed and supervised by an EPLF fighter and her family, who had been recruited from the Solomuna refugee camps. Coro Baraka was strategically located halfway between Port Sudan and the base camps. The large lorries, whose drivers spent the daylight hours sleeping and eating, confining their travel to the nighttime so as to enter Eritrea before sunrise and thus escape detection by Ethiopian MIGs, took twice as long to complete their journey as the Land Cruiser.

After Coro Baraka, the terrain changed dramatically. The sand dunes were replaced by a hard volcanic surface with so many potholes that even our seasoned driver couldn't avoid them all. Despite the renewed supply of morphine, our patient now screamed in even greater agony. This part of the road was probably the most treacherous leg of the journey, where even the sturdiest trucks sometimes broke down. Two years later, to reduce the frequency of breakdowns that were taking their toll on the essential vehicles, the EPLF engineers who specialized in road repair brought their heavy road-building equipment from Eritrea into Sudan every night and back to Eritrea before dawn until they had resurfaced the entire stretch of road with crushed gravel, probably building the best road in all of rural Sudan.

Finally, the driver pointed to the vague silhouette of a mountain range rising from the desert far away and announced with a broad smile that those were the foothills of Eritrea. He was coming home! Now the car began to climb up and down sharp inclines and around the deep craters until we came to a point in the road blocked by a red and white boom: the official border between Sudan and Eritrea.

After the driver had honked several times, two sleepy young men emerged, carrying AK-47 rifles and Israeli hand grenades and dressed in standard EPLF combat gear, khaki shorts, camouflage shirts, homemade plastic sandals, and large white cotton shawls (*kushuk*) that kept them warm in the cold desert night. One stood guard with his Kalashnikov at the ready while the other carefully inspected our passports, visas, and other papers to make sure we were legitimate. When he came to me, he seemed to take an inordinate amount of time comparing my face with my passport picture. After our driver half-jokingly assured them that I wasn't CIA, the guards raised the boom and we passed into Eritrea. But it would still take another three or four hours on increasingly treacherous roads before we would finally reach our destination.

In the meanwhile, the driver had begun to search for something in the pitch-black Sahel flats, but I couldn't imagine what he could possibly find in the darkness. Here and there he briefly stopped the car next to a bush but then moved on. Finally, he appeared to arrive at the bush he had been looking for—although it looked exactly like all the other bushes to me! He turned off his motor, honked his horn, and waited. Finally, a sleepy fighter dressed like the previous guards crawled out from his underground shelter, dragged a heavy rubber hose to the car, and filled our tank with fuel. Our driver and the station manager then compared notes to make sure that the numbers checked. This service station was part of a network of stations distributed throughout the liberated zones to ensure that the urgently needed supplies always reached their destination in time. All the drivers knew exactly where these stations were hidden.

After yet another hour of twisting and turning, our driver stopped for the last time, cheerfully slapped me on the back, and congratulated us both on having safely reached our destination. Then, pointing to the sky, he indicated that it was almost dawn; he was in a hurry to deliver his patient to the Central Hospital before sunrise. Unceremoniously, he threw our luggage on the ground, honked his horn three times, waved to us with a cheery "Good luck!" and disappeared. There we stood, the journalist and I, stranded in the middle of nowhere.

With a sense of relief we finally discovered a flashlight flickering halfway up the mountain and coming toward us. It was the EPLF protocol officer, who checked our passports for the fourth time to make sure that we were who we said we were and then curtly told us to pick up our baggage and follow him up the steep goat path to an opening into the side of the mountain. This was the entrance to the EPLF guesthouse, where all visitors recuperated from their long journey before tending to their various assignments. Inside the cave about ten people were packed together on the ground, snoring peacefully.

As the protocol officer pointed to a spot in the cave where we could unroll our sleeping bags, his flashlight by chance lit up a large poster of the calm, sad face of Brazilian archbishop Dom Helder Camara, who looked down on us with his ironic comment: "When I feed the poor, they call me a saint. When I ask why the poor have no food, they call me a communist." There was no longer any doubt. We had arrived at the base camps of the EPLF. But what was this strange place of sand, rocks, thorn bushes, goats, camels, and freedom fighters?

· 2 ·

A BRIEF OVERVIEW OF MODERN ERITREA

After two days of rest and relaxation in the guesthouse, I realized that if I wanted to understand what made Eritrea's social revolution even possible, and what gave the country's liberation movement its distinctive characteristics, I would have to gain at least some familiarity with Eritrea's people, their culture, its history, and its relations with its neighbors on the Horn of Africa. I would have to see for myself how a small band of ill-equipped Eritrean "terrorists," "bandits," and "counterrevolutionaries," fighting with out-of-date weapons, was able to defeat a conscript army that was ten to fifteen times larger and equipped with all the latest military ordinance—and how these outgunned guerrilla fighters *were at the same time able to rehabilitate and educate thousands of children.* And, specifically, I would need to learn something about how Eritrea's children—and its orphans in particular—managed to cope. I would have to understand how an unforgiving physical environment and the daily experience of war, danger, loss, and chronic privation profoundly affected not only their health and general welfare, but also their social development and capacity for self-reliance (a key to the success of the EPLF).

The Land

The landmass of Eritrea, including about three hundred small islands in the Red Sea, is roughly the size of Pennsylvania (125,000 square kilometers). The country's eastern boundary stretches for 1,200 kilometers along the humid coast and faces the almost unlimited oil fields of the Arabian Peninsula—surely a major source of interest for the European colonial powers. Across its southern border lies Ethiopia, while its northern and western borders are shared with Sudan. The fertile Western Plains that extend into Sudan and the arid Eastern Lowlands surround the Central Highlands, which rise sharply from below sea level to six to seven thousand feet.

Eritrea commands two major ports on the Red Sea, Massawa and Assab. For decades, Ethiopia had coveted these two ports, claiming that, without access to the Red Sea, it could not survive. That claim to a right of access had for many years been the explicit cause of the thirty-year war.

The People

Long before Ethiopia and Eritrea constituted two distinct social and political entities, and long before Middle Eastern and European invaders colonized the Horn of Africa, the inhabitants of the hot, humid Red Sea coast were trading actively with Arabs, Greeks, Romans, Turks, and other seafaring peoples. Their exchange of goods and ideas planted the seeds of a cosmopolitan outlook and mentality that would eventually set them apart from feudal societies in the hinterlands of Ethiopia.

Depending on the source, the population of Eritrea as of early 2016 was estimated to be between 5.3 and 6.7 million, with another million Eritreans living in the diaspora; by contrast, the population of Ethiopia was estimated to be between 94 and 104 million—almost twenty times that of Eritrea! The two largest ethnic groups in Eritrea are the Tigrinya-speaking and Tigre-speaking people, who together account for about 85 percent of the total population. Most Tigrinya people live in the Central Highlands; they come from Coptic Christian (Orthodox or Tewahedo) religious backgrounds and make their living by subsistence farming. A small sector of the Muslim population follows a purely nomadic lifestyle while the others make their living as agro-pastoralists. Most Tigre people inhabit the Western and Eastern Lowlands as well as the Northern Highlands. The remaining 15 percent of the population, including the Afar, Bilen, Nara, Hdareb, Kunama, Rashaida, and Saho minorities, speak one or the other of nine different languages, all derived from four distinct language roots. Until recently, small congregations of Roman Catholics, Protestants, Pentecostals, and Jehovah's Witnesses, as well as a few Jews, were able to practice their religion without any interference, attesting at that time to the tolerance and open-mindedness of the common people to opposing points of view.

The Legal Heritage

As in most rural areas of East Africa, the village had for centuries been the keystone of all economic, social, and civil affairs in the Central Highlands. By the twelfth or thirteenth century, all customary laws pertaining to land tenure, property rights, the rights of women and children, marriage, inheritance, minor infractions, theft, homicide, and the like were permanently recorded in "The Book"—the *Highi Endaba* or "Laws of the Fathers." Since the customary laws were written for the Tigrinya-speaking communities in the Central Highlands, they were written in Tigrinya, the language of the common people—the peasants and students who would in time become the leaders in the country's struggle for independence.

To keep the customary laws current, The Book was regularly updated. Proposed changes were written on separate pieces of parchment and pasted into the appropriate pages with cactus latex. On the one hand, The Book was therefore a permanent record of customary laws that were never discarded despite fears that they might interfere with social progress. On the other hand, it was a "dynamic" living document that linked the past to the present and the future.

Asmarom Legesse, a renowned professor of cultural anthropology specializing in East African cultures, has called attention to the unique role that The Book plays in the social and economic lives of the farmers: "The most fascinating aspect of the Eritrean Customary Law is its dynamism. In the Eritrean context, laws are not written in order to be administered by law enforcement agencies. Laws exist as a background to intervention, to mediation, to conflict resolution. Conflict resolution is the most important aspect of Eritrean Customary Law."[1] In other words, all important decisions were made by an elected village council after long discussion and consensus building rather than by simply imposing the will of the majority on the overturned minority.

The Economic and Social Tradition

The Diesa system of land tenure that was practiced primarily in the Central Highlands left a lasting impact on the rural communities. Although it went through a number of transformations, the system dates back at least to the Middle Ages and is anchored in the basic premise that the land belongs to the community, not to any landlord or village chief, and that neither individuals nor individual families are allowed to sell it to outsiders. The land was divided into equal-size plots that were graded on a three-point scale according to their fertility, and each household was entitled to an equal share:[2] one plot at each level of fertility.

Each family had the right to cultivate and harvest its three plots for a period of seven years, after which the rights and responsibilities of tilling, planting, cultivating, and harvesting the three fields were transferred to another family for the next seven years. A village committee supervised the redistribution of the land. As long as every household in the village respected the rules of periodic land transfer and gave its particular plots of arable land the proper attention throughout their tenure, the village prospered. But if one household neglected the land during its tenure so that it would no longer be able to benefit from the next year's crops, first one family and then another and another would also begin to neglect the land. In time, the system of land tenure based on shared responsibility and benefits would collapse, and everyone would lose. Thus, under the Diesa system, each family had a personal stake in cooperating to meet the needs of the community.

It was a primitive form of socialism, but it had worked for centuries and seemed to be reflected in the community's attitudes toward its children. Rather than viewing children as if they were the private property of their parents and were not to be interfered with by strangers, society viewed children as everyone's responsibility, and the same enlightened self-interest that sustained the system of land tenure also made it incumbent upon all adults to safeguard all the village children and monitor their behavior. On the crowded streets of Asmara, perfect strangers didn't hesitate to scold or, if necessary, slap the face of any child who had run recklessly through the fast-moving traffic; nor did they shy away from pulling the ear of a bully who was beating a younger child or from picking up and comforting the child who had been teased by a gang of older children. There was no tort law, and no need for a tort law, to punish offending adults for overstepping their bounds and meting out discipline or providing solace to another parent's child if the occasion warranted interference.

As the towns and cities became urbanized and historical changes in the rest of the world reverberated in Eritrea, it was perhaps inevitable that the strong social bonds afforded by the Diesa system would weaken. After independence, the Diesa system was no longer economically efficient or profitable, and the land was nationalized. However, the social bonds persisted and continued to influence the sense of community responsibility toward children.

The Historical Perspective and Seeds of Resistance

In 1880, Italian forces took over Eritrea, holding it for sixty years. They built their colonial capital in the Central Highlands on top of Asmara, a long-abandoned village dating back to the eleventh century. The colonial administration exploited Eritrea's natural wealth, cheap labor, agricultural resources, and industrial potential, as well as the genius of its people, to build factories, where it introduced modern techniques of mass production and agriculture for export to Italy. The port facilities in Massawa were modernized, and excellent all-weather roads and bridges—still a marvel of engineering today—were constructed throughout the Central Highlands. Italian engineers also built a narrow-track railroad that climbed up over 7,600 feet from sea level in Massawa, passing through more than twenty-five tunnels before reaching Asmara. The Italians, throughout their occupation of the land, trained the Eritrean workers in various industrial, administrative, and agricultural skills, unintentionally creating a class-conscious, technically sophisticated, and politically savvy urban labor force that would eventually be converted into a full-fledged army fighting for independence against colonial and neocolonial oppressors.

In 1935, Italian dictator Benito Mussolini invaded and occupied Ethiopia, hoping to establish a Second Roman Empire in East Africa, with Asmara as its capital. Six years later, in World War II, the British seized Eritrea, drove the Italians out, and administered the country as a UN trust territory until 1950. While there, they abolished racist laws; encouraged the formation of political parties and labor unions; and built new hospitals, public health clinics, schools, and factories.

After the war, the question arose about what to do with the former Italian colonies in East Africa. Libya and Italian Somaliland were granted independence after a brief period of UN trusteeship. But Eritrea proved to be a thorny problem: Haile Selassie, Ethiopia's emperor, claimed Eritrea as part of Ethiopia, while the Eritreans themselves were sharply divided as to whether they wanted union with Ethiopia, federation status, or total independence as a sovereign nation. Finally, in 1952, the UN called for the federation of Eritrea with Ethiopia. Under this resolution, Eritrea would maintain its own administrative and legal structure and have control over its own domestic affairs, while the federal government, under Haile Selassie, would control its foreign affairs. But the emperor, who hoped to appropriate Eritrea as the fourteenth province of Ethiopia, was not satisfied with this arrangement. Seeking to crush Eritrea's aspirations for independence, he decreed that Amharic, the official language of Ethiopia, would henceforth be the only language of instruction allowed in any Eritrean classroom. This put Eritrean students at a great disadvantage, as Tigrinya, the most common language in Eritrea, could no longer be used in schools. Then, compounding the insult and humiliation, Selassie further ordered that all books written in Tigrinya—perhaps Eritrea's greatest cultural treasure—be burned in public.

Rising up in resistance to the emperor's imperialistic encroachment, Eritrean youth organized mass demonstrations throughout the city and boycotted the schools. In 1958 Eritrea's labor unions called a general strike, probably the first time in modern history that such an explicitly political action had occurred in all of Africa. In response, the emperor ordered the Eritrean police to fire on the crowd, killing several peaceful civilian protestors. A delegation of outraged Eritreans took their grievance to both the UN and the International Court of Justice in The Hague, but the UN remained silent and the Court did nothing. Having exhausted all diplomatic remedies, the people of Eritrea started an armed rebellion, hoping that such desperate measures would finally get the attention of the UN General Assembly. But in 1962, Ethiopia dissolved the Eritrean parliament and annexed the country, precipitating a bloody war that would last for thirty years until Eritrea finally achieved its independence.

The first serious group to mount an organized armed resistance was the Eritrean Liberation Front (ELF). By 1970, however, a small group of ELF combatants—no more than thirty—had become increasingly disillusioned with the group's ineffective military strategies, its flawed political programs, and especially its corrupt personal practices. After several failed attempts at reform, these dissidents broke away and formed a new opposition group, the Eritrean People's Liberation Front (EPLF).

The political differences between the ELF and EPLF hardened, resulting in a fruitless civil war that persisted until the peasants, fed up with the pointless bloodshed, sent village elders to the command structures of both factions, scolding them for their inane squabbling and urging them to stop killing each other and focus on the fight for independence. The leaders took heed and tried to reconcile their differences in pursuit of their common goal. But the EPLF, having succeeded in marginalizing the ELF, then concentrated its sparse resources on defeating the Ethiopian armies. By 1978, almost all of the country had been liberated from Ethiopia except the major cities and a few isolated garrisons.

In the meantime, Soviet generals had replaced some of the Ethiopian generals and directed the campaigns, and East German advisors suddenly appeared in the Ethiopian trenches. Yemen, which had once supported the Eritrean cause, sent its experienced pilots to fly bombing and strafing missions over Eritrea, and Israeli commandos trained Ethiopian assault troops. In short, Eritrea was reduced to an orphan state. And when it became clear that a small ragtag army of bandits and "ultra-leftists" might actually defeat the Ethiopian army and embarrass the Soviet Union, hundreds of the latest Soviet tanks, the fear-inspiring *katyushas* ("Stalin Organs"), MIG fighter jets, and helicopter gunships came out of nowhere and overwhelmed the EPLF.

The massive Ethiopian offensive might have broken the will of most independence movements, but the EPLF began the long, strategic retreat to the Northern Highlands, finally regrouping in Sahel Province. Those who participated in the retreat described in detail the remarkable discipline of the combatants. Casualties were kept to a minimum; hospitalized combatants were carried to safety in lorries, in abandoned Ethiopian tanks, and—under the most desperate conditions—on the backs of hospital personnel and recovering fighters. Nearly all captured technical and military equipment and essential supplies were salvaged. Small cells of guerrilla fighters stayed behind to fight rearguard actions, infiltrate the large cities for intelligence operations, and serve as advance commandos. The deep canyons of Sahel Province offered the retreating army an ideal haven that Soviet tanks and advanced Soviet MIGs couldn't penetrate.

Rather than succumbing to a sense of defeat, the EPLF leadership reevaluated its successes and failures over the two decades, modified its military strategies, and refined its social program of prospective nation building.

Notes

1 As cited by Issayas Kemey, *Issayas' Blog*, January 11, 2014, http://kemey.blogspot.com/2014/01/a-conversation-with-solomon-tsehaye_11.html
2 Dan Connell and Tom Killion, *Historical Dictionary of Eritrea*, 2nd ed. (Lanham, Md.: Scarecrow Press, 2010), 178.

· 3 ·

THE BASE CAMPS

All foreign visitors to the base camps spent the first day or two in the EPLF guesthouse to recover from their arduous journey, get used to the eerie vibrations of the sand migrating from one dune to the next, and be briefed once more about what was and was not safe to do in this totally alien environment. Early on the morning after our arrival, the journalist and I were invited to a breakfast of sweetened tea, local bread, cheese from Holland, and a large pot of strawberry jam from Belgium. These were a gift from Dr. Nerayo Teklemichael, a pediatrician in charge of the Eritrean Public Health Program, who made frequent official visits to Europe and, whenever possible, brought back assorted delicacies donated by European NGOs for the hospitalized combatants and lost children.

After breakfast, I got my first glimpse of the place where the driver had deposited us the night before. The desert stretched out in all directions to the edges of the steep cliffs of barren red stone that kept out the Russian-Ethiopian enemy tanks. The drought in the Northern Highlands had lasted for more than four years. Everything seemed dead except the swirling clouds of sand stirred by the hot desert winds. Even the huge, gnarled baobab trees that had survived here for centuries were now dying.

But the desert was far from dead. Here and there a tuft of grass had squeezed its way through the barren rocks, a symbol of the resistance. Flocks of yellow bowerbirds were busy building their nests in the trees that surrounded the guesthouse. At sunrise, the sad song of the mourning doves announced another hot day without any rain.

After we had rested for a full day and the journalists (there were now three more, from Atlanta, Georgia, who were also staying in the guesthouse) had gathered information about the current status in the trenches, the protocol officer assembled the newcomers for another crash course in basic survival skills. He warned us that the moment we heard the high-pitched screech of a MIG jet, we should stand absolutely still and not try to run for cover; this is because the Ethiopian pilots were flying at such a high speed that they could only detect movement. Since all the combatants and most of the nomads heeded this advice, casualty rates among humans were low but relatively high among the goats and camels.

Eventually, one journalist asked the question that was on every visitor's mind—namely, how could we pay our hosts for transportation, food, lodging, and hospitality? The protocol officer dismissed the question with a wave of his hand, noting that we were guests of the Front. He did, however, casually mention that the EPLF always needed hard currency and would welcome any donation in U.S. dollars or British pounds that could easily be traded for essential supplies on the black market in Khartoum. To underscore his suggestion, he explained that the combatants were all volunteers who had surrendered their worldly possessions, including money, watches, jewels, books, and extra clothing, upon joining the Front; these possessions were equally distributed to each, according to his or her need.

By four o'clock in the afternoon, it was safe to travel and time for us to get on with our various assignments. The journalists all knew exactly where they wanted to go—to the trenches, where there was action. While I wasn't at all keen on joining them, I envied them their clarity of purpose. I still didn't have the slightest idea what I was supposed to be doing in Eritrea until the protocol officer informed me that, as a doctor, I was expected in the Central Hospital. He put me in the back of a truck, together with an emaciated cow and the grizzled skeleton of a man. The man, who had been fighting Ethiopians most of his life, was now returning to the field for the surgical removal of a malignant tumor in his jaw; he had full confidence in the EPLF doctors, but wasn't sure he could trust the Sudanese doctors in Khartoum.

No sooner had I arrived at the Central Hospital than a lively young woman nicknamed "La Italiana" welcomed me effusively as if I were a long-lost friend or relative. She had worked in Italy as a scullery maid for several years, but, having become fed up with the life of a servant, left Italy and joined the EPLF, where she was now a free spirit who no longer had to wet-mop other people's bathroom floors. Alerted by field radio that I was on my way, she had prepared the guest room, which was lavishly furnished with a real bed, a real mattress, a real pillow—and a flush toilet that didn't work.

While I was waiting in the guest room to see what would happen next, a tall, handsome man dressed in fatigues and plastic sandals and sporting an unloaded automatic pistol appeared silently out of the darkness. With a broad smile, he welcomed me to the Orotta Central Hospital and introduced himself in perfect English as Dr. Assefaw Tekeste, one of the surgeons and the doctor in charge of medical services for the civilian population in the base camps of the liberated zones. After inspecting my bedroom to ensure that La Italiana had done her job, he showed me the outdoor cafeteria—a circle of rocks under one of the few shade trees—where I could take my breakfast in the morning. The cafeteria was the domain of a totally self-assured, fun-loving older woman who cracked jokes whenever possible. She looked after all the surgeons, treating them with the solicitude of a mother hen to make sure that, after far too many hours of surgery, they at least got enough to eat. Although I still had no idea what would be expected of me after all these elaborate preparations for my well-being, in less than four hours after leaving the guesthouse, I felt at home.

The next morning, Assefaw invited me to join him on medical rounds and a tour of the hospital. Often described as the "longest hospital in the world," Orotta's many heavily camouflaged wards meandered along a dry riverbed for anywhere between four and six kilometers (depending on who was counting). These wards were caves that had been gouged deep into the sides of the cliffs and then reinforced by wooden beams to protect the patients from all but the heaviest aerial bombardments. The surgical and orthopedic wards were filled with battle casualties: gaping abdominal wounds, amputations, head injuries, severe lacerations, arm and leg fractures, and napalm burns. The medical wards were full of young women and their children, as well as old men barely able to sit up in bed and suffering from malnutrition, chronic heart disease, dehydration, malaria, tuberculosis, Leishmaniasis, and other parasitic diseases.

One of the wards, which stood somewhat apart from the others, specialized in the surgical treatment of glaucoma and cataracts. Bilateral cataracts were very common in the bright sunlight at this altitude. Once the Surgical Department began to receive large shipments of lens implants from Australian friends of the EPLF, the surgeons were able to restore the sight of large numbers of civilians and selected combatants who could function easily even with limited vision.

A few blind combatants with patches over both eyes were practicing how to navigate around in this rocky and unpredictable terrain. With the help of a cane and a barefoot doctor, they practiced walking all day long and laughed it off when they fell or bumped into each other.

The Obstetrics Department was equipped with two old-fashioned incubators for premature infants; the incubators had somehow been wrested from the Ethiopian army, but they were essentially useless because the electrical heating elements that were supposed to keep the infants warm were burned out, and the Engineering Department didn't have the spare parts to fix the incubators. Perhaps it would take another raid on the enormous Ethiopian supply depots to secure a functioning incubator for premature infants in the base camps.

The three operating theaters were housed in carefully camouflaged metal containers and powered by dedicated generators that the EPLF had trucked in all the way from Port Sudan. Especially after major battles, the generators ran all night and, if necessary, well into the early daylight hours to keep the battle casualties alive. Acute combat casualties always had the highest priority, but when there was a lull in the fighting, the surgeons performed elective procedures on combatants and civilians alike.

Many of the older civilians in the rural areas had for years been crippled by rheumatic heart disease but couldn't be sent abroad for definitive surgical treatment (valvulotomy) because of the costs. At the request of the EPLF, a French cardiac surgeon had come to the field to show the local surgeons how one might perform open-heart surgery with ether as the only available anesthesia and without any bottled oxygen. First the visiting surgeon demonstrated how to perform a valvulotomy on several cardiac patients while his Eritrean colleagues watched. Then he and a young Eritrean doctor who had recently returned from the Soviet Union performed several operations together, the French doctor guiding the Eritrean doctor into the heart until the novice demonstrated that he knew how to operate alone while his French counterpart watched in case anything went wrong. That was the kind of foreign aid the EPLF welcomed and valued most because it didn't make them dependent on outside sources. Over the years, a number of other European specialty surgeons had come to the base camps and trained Eritrean doctors in their specialized surgical skills, often leaving their instruments behind for use in the field.

Our next stop was at another carefully camouflaged surgical ward that looked pretty much like the other ones, except that someone had gone to a great deal of trouble to decorate the entrance with colorful beds of fresh flowers—something unheard of in the harsh environment of Sahel Province. That somebody who had made the desert bloom turned out to be Dr. Leinash, Assefaw's wife and a fully trained dental surgeon, who had taken postgraduate training in maxillofacial surgery in Bulgaria before joining the Front and now was in charge of reconstructive and restorative surgery. The surgical ward was filled with combatants with terribly disfiguring facial injuries, shot-off jaws, gaping wounds, and faces burned into terrible grimaces that were no longer recognizably human. Some of their injuries were so extensive that the patients could no longer use their mouths to speak or eat and had to be fed by gastric tube. Nevertheless, Dr. Leinash worked her magic on these terribly disfigured faces by using bone grafts, full-thickness pedicle grafts, and whatever else any Western maxillofacial surgeon would require, and she performed these miracles in an environment where operating conditions were far from ideal.

Right next door to the surgical ward where she worked, Dr. Leinash had assembled a fully equipped laboratory for making serviceable dentures so that combatants whose faces had been healed could now speak comprehensibly. In the same series of underground bunkers, she had also assembled a more conventional outpatient facility with two dental chairs; here, she and two assistants treated toothaches, constructed dental crowns, built dental bridges, and filled cavities for everyone in the base camps as well as for the civilians living in the surrounding hills. But she never forgot her flowers.

Half a kilometer "downstream" on the other side of the dry riverbed was a large, camouflaged shipping container. With the help of the Civil Engineering Department, Melles Seyum, a clinical laboratory diagnostician from the EPLF, had converted the metal container into a sophisticated clinical laboratory, where he had assembled what looked like all the essential components for the analysis of whole blood, platelets, serum, sputum, urine, and feces—components that are essential for a proper diagnosis of the chronic and acute illnesses likely to be encountered in this part of the world.

A small icebox maintained by a small kerosene heater was able to store a few pints of whole blood for a short while, but the refrigerator was unreliable, and too much of the blood spoiled before it could be used. So the Engineering

Department experimented with alternative sources of electricity to power a refrigerator that had also been freed from the Ethiopian storage facilities. Wind-powered turbines would have been relatively easy to set up, and solar energy was never in short supply, but both turbines and conventional solar panels were much too easy to spot from the air and were therefore unacceptable. Eventually, two Australian environmental engineers discovered how to reduce the glare of the solar panels. A year later, an array of solar panels with a relatively low reflectance was installed, generating enough electricity to power a large refrigerator that could now safely store enough whole blood to meet most of the needs of wounded fighters as well as civilians.

On another evening after the sun had set, one of the pharmacists invited me to visit the famous underground pharmacy that already had an international reputation for excellence. Every night, an army of pharmacists and their assistants descended into the bowels of the earth, put on sterile gowns, masks, and hairnets, and spent the night producing a great variety of essential drugs in rigorously controlled isolation rooms. The sophisticated machines required to mass-produce medicines that would meet rigorous industry standards on the open market had been donated by Eritrea support groups in Australia, Belgium, Germany, Norway, and the United Kingdom. At the time of my first visit in 1985, the underground pharmacy was already producing the fifty essential drugs recommended by the World Health Organization. Every drug was checked for hardness, solubility, and bioavailability and then widely distributed by barefoot doctors throughout the liberated zones and to peasants living in the contested areas.

Intravenous (IV) fluids were also essential for the treatment and recovery of severely wounded combatants, other surgical patients, and children with diarrhea, cholera, and upper respiratory infections, but the fluids had to be imported in prepackaged form at great expense, and their delivery from Port Sudan was often delayed. Since IV fluids are nothing more mysterious than distilled water, ordinary table salt, and sugar, the EPLF's Medical Department decided to make its own. Again, European friends came to the rescue and donated the necessary mixing machines, filters, and sterilizers for the mass production of fluids that met industry standards of chemical composition and purity. The carpentry shop built a series of rabbit cages so that each batch of fluids could also be tested for sterility and pyrogenicity (causing fever) before it could be poured into plastic bags for distribution to all the health stations.

However, the plastic bags first had to be imported from Port Sudan before they could be filled and distributed. It didn't take the Medical Department very long to hit on a sustainable and reliable solution. For several years the EPLF had been producing plastic sandals for all combatants. The Engineering Department discovered a way to modify the sandal machine until it produced sandals for half the year and plastic IV bags for the other half. Both plastic bags and plastic sandals were now available year-round.

When Andu had been preparing me for my first trip to the EPLF base camps, he had stressed repeatedly that what the combatants, especially the leaders, wanted most were books—books on primary health care, public health, surgery, radiology, internal medicine, pediatrics, and obstetrics-gynecology—whatever I could carry. Among the books that I was sure would be most welcome was *Where There Is No Doctor*,[1] probably the most well-known volume in a growing series. Written and published during the many liberation struggles in Central America, it was now a critical resource in creating the teaching aids, educational cartoons, and posters in the many EPLF schools that taught the youngsters the importance of personal hygiene and exhorted them to brush their teeth and wash their faces and hands. Teachers emphasized public health lessons on preventable diseases and released primary health messages about hygiene, protected water sources, and preventing trachoma. These lessons were all kept safe in the Orotta library, a cave dug deep into one of the surrounding hills. When I proudly presented Assefaw with two copies of the book, he smiled, thanked me, excused himself, and came back a few minutes later carrying the same book that had already been translated into Tigrinya and was now mass produced for distribution among the nurses and doctors in the field.

Perhaps the most remarkable publishing venture was a threeway dictionary in Tigrinya, Arabic, and English that had been written and assembled in the field, bound and published abroad, and was now widely distributed. What kind of revolutionaries were these bandits and gangsters who read, translated, and compiled very thick textbooks in their underground library when they weren't fighting Soviet tanks and Ethiopian MIGs, stitching up mangled bodies, or debating what was left of their liberationist ideology now that the Soviet Union, which had earlier backed them, had betrayed them and joined the neocolonial Ethiopian enemy?

One morning before sunrise, Assefaw invited me to join him for an inspection tour of several frontline hospitals so that I could see how such hospitals function under fire. An unexpected air raid interrupted our trip, forcing us to duck into a cave that the EPLF often used as an air raid shelter. As we adapted to the dark, we saw that we were not alone: sharing the cave with us were an old truck driver, two local farmers, and one ex-EPLF fighter who must have been at least seventy. They had been surprised by the unusual time of the air raid, and we were all now huddled together, waiting for the all-clear signal.

But just sitting there doing nothing was anathema for Assefaw, who had an uncanny knack of turning almost any social situation into an opportunity to learn and teach without ever becoming a bore. Here in the cave, he argued persuasively that since we had to wait until the Ethiopian MIG had left, this might be a good opportunity for me to tell the others something about recent advances in our understanding of brain development, which Assefaw and I had sometimes discussed during the long nights when it was hard to sleep. But I couldn't imagine that anything I could say on this subject could possibly interest our four cave mates, none of whom had ever gone to school or learned to read. Nor did I know very much about the subject. But Assefaw reminded me that I had gone to good schools and universities for many years and undoubtedly knew more about brain development than anyone else in the cave. He also reminded me that it was the obligation of those who know to share their knowledge so as to enable those who never had the advantage of an education to learn and understand as well. No one had ever put it to me so clearly, although I should have been able to figure it out for myself.

So I searched for topics in brain development that were well circumscribed, and I eventually settled on programmed cell death and synaptic pruning, counterintuitive concepts that nevertheless refer to essential mechanisms of normal brain development. Even today we generally take it for granted that normal brain development is characterized by the growth, proliferation, increased complexity of organization, and so forth—in other words, that *more is better*. Yet in some aspects of brain development, synaptic pruning is essential for the development of normal brain function, and when it does not occur, the brain will not function properly. In other words, sometimes *less is better*. For the next half hour, I therefore held forth on programmed cell death as a prerequisite for normal brain development while Assefaw translated back and forth between English and Tigrinya and the MIG overhead kept searching for suitable targets.

To Assefaw's satisfaction and my surprise, the idea of programmed cell death stirred up a lively discussion and many interesting questions, most of which I managed to answer. But then the truck driver asked, "What does this programmed cell death have to do with our revolution?" I thought it was his polite way of telling me that he was bored and wanted to change the subject, but Assefaw assured me that the driver had asked the question in all seriousness and expected and deserved a serious answer. I was stumped. Having grown up in a world with very different *a priori* assumptions, I wasn't prepared to accept that whatever promotes the liberation struggle is worth knowing, and that whatever doesn't, isn't. But the truck driver's question came up again and again whenever Assefaw asked me to give a lecture on some esoteric topic, and it was a question for which I never found a satisfactory answer.

As we continued our tour, the surprises kept piling up. A large carpentry shop, staffed mostly by amputees, was producing a mountain of artificial legs and arms. Next door, an underground garage was revulcanizing the huge tires that had been taken from the Ethiopian army and its Soviet advisors. In another underground garage, skilled auto mechanics were repairing the large trucks—the lifeline of the EPLF—that had been damaged during the arduous nightly trek from Port Sudan. And in yet another such garage, mechanics supervised the repair of some of the latest Soviet tanks that the EPLF had captured, modifying them to their own needs and making sure that the turret guns pointed in the right direction.

Down the road a little further, a crew of technicians armed with magnifying glasses was huddled over a long table, repairing a wealth of watches, shortwave radios, and other electronic equipment. These items were to be distributed throughout the base camps until every combatant had a working wristwatch, and everyone at least had access to local and international news transmitted by the excellent Japanese shortwave radios that the EPLF had liberated from Ethiopian warehouses scattered throughout occupied and liberated Eritrea.

Of all the cottage industries and services that had sprung up in the bunkers of the EPLF base camps, perhaps the one that impressed me the most seemed far removed from liberation struggles and yet of great importance for human dignity. In a modest underground factory, six or seven combatants were rolling what looked like surgical bandages. On closer inspection, however, they weren't surgical bandages at all. These workers were mass-producing enough sanitary napkins to meet the needs of combatants and civilians living in the liberated zone.

Mass-producing sanitary napkins didn't fit my picture of what of freedom fighters do, but it showed me how much I still had to learn about Eritrea's revolution. For centuries, superstition had forced menstruating women to hide in shame in their tents and squat over filthy rags. Years later, after independence, I heard that Muslim women had been so impressed by the convenience of sanitary napkins that they now insisted that local dry goods stores always carry a supply. By this simple innovation, the EPLF had brought about a cultural change and secured a newfound dignity for Eritrea's girls and women.

Note

1 David Werner, with Carol Thuman and Jane Maxwell, *Where There Is No Doctor: A Village Health Care Handbook* (Berkeley, Calif.: Hesperian Health Guides, 1977).

· 4 ·

THE HUMAN FACTOR

Many authoritative books, journals, and formal reports have been written about Eritrea's colonial history, its thirty-year war for independence from Ethiopia, and its goal of building a democratic society.[1] Yet, with a few exceptions,[2] most of these publications make only a passing reference to the silent courage, personal commitment, and self-discipline of the individual combatants—the human factor that made this extraordinary experiment in nation-building possible. This was the essential ingredient not just for military success, but even more so, for at least one successful social revolution in the graveyard of so many failed revolutions.

Historians and political scientists might reasonably argue that personal motivations, ambitions, aspirations, thoughts, ruminations, fears, acts of courage or cowardice, and feelings of shame and regret all make up what I have here called, for want of a better term, the human factor. Expert analysts in the social sciences contend that there is no room for such undefined constructs as "the human factor" when trying to understand such momentous counterintuitive events as the defeat of an Ethiopian Goliath by an Eritrean David, and perhaps they are right. On the other hand, they may not be as right as their rigorous theories might have led them to believe.

I was convinced at the time, and I am still convinced, that the human factor, elusive as it may be, plays a far greater role in the dynamics of historical change than we are inclined to believe. For example, it seems obvious, at least to me, that it was essentially the human factor that had befuddled the best and the brightest American statesmen[3] in their vain attempts to orchestrate the Vietnam War by bombing North Vietnam back to the Stone Age. Despite overwhelming weapons superiority, fleets of helicopter gunships, saturation bombing, and the use of napalm, they simply couldn't figure out a way to defeat the Viet Cong.

And so, perhaps it was the same human factor that frustrated the Ethiopian generals and their Soviet advisors when they had to concede that Eritrean bandits, rebels, traitors, and leftists had defeated an Ethiopian army ten times larger, backed up by advanced Soviet tanks and MIG-15s. Elusive as it no doubt is, it may also be the same human factor that will one day be transferred from the current generation of Eritrean freedom fighters to the next generation, with the mission of consolidating the freedoms gained as a result of armed struggle.

But if we want to know now what it was that made the impossible possible, learning about the experience of the combatants as they sweated and bled through the everyday chaos of battle might bring us one step closer to understanding the elusive human factor. At least that was what I had in mind after explaining to a few of the English-speaking combatants why I was interested in hearing about their personal motivations for and reactions to being in the front lines.

Nearly all of them were willing, often even eager, to tell me about their revolution, about the battle strategies and tactical maneuvers of the EPLF, about how the EPLF acquired its weapons and supplies, and about the great courage shown and sacrifices made by their comrades. But the moment I crossed the line and intruded into their personal realm—how they themselves felt at the moment of truth, why they had not run away when the dreaded helicopter gunships raked their trenches, why they hadn't given up after the strategic retreat—they simply didn't answer. It was as if either they had not understood what I was asking or such apparently innocuous questions about their backgrounds, their families, and so forth were strictly taboo. I wanted to ask about what they had experienced of danger as children; that is, what was it about the young people of Eritrea that made them seem indifferent to danger, which is how they appeared to me. But, for all sorts of reasons, of which I discovered only a few—and perhaps in large measure because we communicated through the filter of a translator—they wouldn't talk about themselves. And mostly they were all puzzled as to why anyone, and particularly a stranger from a foreign culture and language, would ask such intrusive (and rather stupid) questions.

Nevertheless, some of them did get the drift of my questions and tried to satisfy my curiosity (or what they took for curiosity) without violating their personal privacy. Some of them, for example, explained that people from the highlands had all been raised in a traditional culture that highly prized modesty and self-effacement, and they still felt contempt for anyone who boasted, showed off, promoted himself ahead of others, or even had a tendency to dominate the social situation by talking too much (what in the United States during the 60s and 70s was referred to as "ego-tripping"). Getting high marks on school examinations was highly valued from early primary school, yet the children were routinely chastised, scolded, or even physically punished when they spoke excessively about any personal accomplishments that would make them stand out from the crowd. If I had understood correctly what the combatants told me about the issue, praising the collective over the individual had been part of the village morality long before "the collective" became a political buzzword. Especially now that so many of their friends had been killed, even talking about themselves as individuals rather than as the collective "we" would, they felt, dishonor the memory of their comrades. Thus, pride—fear of being suspected by their comrades of cowardly thoughts if not of cowardly actions—became a serious liability for the squad.

Perhaps I had posed these personal questions from the wrong—that is, a Western—perspective. Perhaps the source of their incredible strength, courage, resilience, and self-reliance didn't reside in the individual fighter but was, in fact, inherent in the solidarity of the collective when its members shared a common belief system and a common goal.

One night, Assefaw took me out to one of the small hospitals on the front lines so I could see how the military hospitals functioned. It would take at least two to three hours before we reached our destination, and there were only the two of us in the car. Therefore, I felt it was an auspicious occasion for me to ask Assefaw "my question," even if I might never find out the reason for my obsession with it.

What I knew about Assefaw was that he had grown up in a prominent and well-to-do family in the Central Highlands, in what he half-jokingly considered the best village in all of Eritrea. His father had been an official in the Eritrean parliament during the federation with Ethiopia. So I wondered what had motivated him and his fellow students at Haile Selassie University in Addis Ababa to join a clandestine political opposition group that well might sooner or later land them in Ethiopian prisons? Why had he, who had come from a privileged stratum of Eritrean society, joined a ragtag collection of poorly educated rebels to fight a war of independence when almost no one really believed that such a war could be won? Had his studies convinced him that a Leninist or Maoist revolution would eventually achieve for Eritrea the kind of socialist state for which too many of his friends had already given their lives?

And why had he traded in his prestigious position as surgeon in the most modern hospital in all of Eritrea in order to join the EPLF, sleeping on rocks with snakes and scorpions, hunting for body lice, eating crusts of dry bread when it was available, having no clean water to drink, and facing death every day? Was he convinced that the social revolution taking place in the base camps of the EPLF would eventually prevail? Or was it perhaps a fierce nationalism that filled the ideological vacuum after the Soviet Union turned its massive artillery and helicopter gunships on its former socialist "comrades"?

By then I thought I knew Assefaw well enough to be certain that he was too honest to hide behind ideological smokescreens or indulge in propaganda that he himself didn't believe. But, like the other combatants, he didn't answer my question. Instead he mentioned that he too had often wondered what the combatants in the front lines thought about as they prepared for the next battle, which some of them wouldn't survive. He was convinced that the unwavering courage that the combatants showed under fire was neither crude bravado nor slavish adulation of ideological abstractions, although a veneer of correct slogans might have served them as a convenient rationalization. They all wanted to live; they all wanted to get married; they all wanted to have children; they all wanted to be left in peace. But they had put their lives on the line to protect their families and villages and to preserve their country's independence.

Assefaw also didn't give away any clues as to what had made him decide to join the Front, with all its known and unknown dangers. Perhaps I had no right to ask him such a personal question. In any case, he deftly turned the question around by asking me what had motivated *me*, an American doctor with a sizable family, a large house, and a cushy job at a good university, to come to this dangerous corner of the world and allow himself to be subjected to the indignities of an impossible climate, an incomprehensible language, and indigestible food? Not being as clever at evading personal questions as

Assefaw, I groped around for answers but they all sounded pretentious, contrived, or both. But we agreed by our silence that there are important questions that cry out to be asked, even if they can never be answered to anyone's satisfaction.

Notes

1. See, for example, Bereket Habte Selassie, *The Making of the Eritrean Constitution: The Dialectic of Process and Substance* (Lawrenceville, NJ: Red Sea Press, 2003); Dan Connell, *Against All Odds: A Chronicle of the Eritrean Revolution with a New Afterword on the Postwar Transition* (Lawrenceville, NJ: Red Sea Press, 1997); James Firebrace, with Stuart Holland, *Never Kneel Down: Drought, Development and Liberation in Eritrea* (Nottingham, UK: Spokesman for War on Want, 1984); Les Gottesman, *To Fight and Learn: The Praxis and Promise of Literacy in Eritrea's Independence War* (Lawrenceville, NJ: Red Sea Press, 1998); Roy Pateman, *Eritrea: Even the Stones Are Burning*, rev. ed. (Lawrenceville, NJ: Red Sea Press, 1998); and David Pool, *From Guerrillas to Government: The Eritrean People's Liberation Front* (Athens: Ohio University Press, 2001).
2. See especially Michela A. Wrong, *I Didn't Do It for You: How the World Betrayed a Small African Nation* (New York: HarperCollins, 2005).
3. See David Halberstam, *The Best and the Brightest* (New York: Random House, 1972).

· 5 ·

DEPARTURES

My visit to the base camp ended abruptly one afternoon when Dr. Nerayo came to tell me to get my gear together and be ready to leave for Port Sudan. There were rumors that the Ethiopian army was preparing for another major offensive, and all traffic in and out of Eritrea would soon stop. A space had been reserved for me on the last truck leaving that afternoon.

As we walked to the staging area to depart, Nerayo told me how much it had meant for him and for many other fighters to get a fresh perspective on the Eritrean revolution. But there was also something else on his mind. He apologized for the blunt and brusque behavior of the combatants: they never said "please" or "thank you" because they took it for granted that everything belonged to everybody, that everyone's responsibility was the responsibility of the community, and that cooperation and mutual help are always expected.[1] But they didn't mean to give offense. It was simply the EPLF style of social interaction that had developed in the field over many years of combat and had become an integral part of the EPLF subculture.

I couldn't reply because I didn't have the slightest idea what he was talking about. All the people I had met in the field had always made me feel welcome. If anything, they had embarrassed me by bending over backward to make my time in the camp comfortable, to help me when I needed help, to be patient with my limitations when I lagged behind, to see that I got the best and most digestible foods to eat, and to ensure that I was safe. While it was patently obvious that I wasn't yet toughened up to their standards, they appeared to accept me for what I was.

Although it seemed paradoxical, I wondered whether Nerayo might be alluding to American sensibilities about race, prejudice, and so forth. I could well understand that there must be thousands of reasons why African Americans growing up in the United States would never be able to forget the brute fact that I was "white" and they were "black." But that couldn't be what Nerayo was talking about. Even during my first visit I was impressed by the fact that the notion of race simply didn't enter into any of our relationships; it wasn't an issue for them, and so it wasn't an issue for me, either.

Perhaps Nerayo had in mind that these brave and imperturbable people who had lived in the trenches with death as a constant companion for the past twenty years no longer had any patience with the niceties of polite conversation; that they rarely said "please" or "thank you" because it might sound like begging. But then Nerayo emphasized that the combatants would only say "thank you" on the rare occasions when the situation called for it, and then only when the meaning of the phrase transcended polite conversation.

He urged me to come back to the field whenever I could, assuring me that I would always be welcome. I gladly accepted his invitation, but said that I wouldn't even consider eating their food, drinking their suwa (a traditional alcoholic beverage made up of water and bread and fermented for thirteen days), or wasting their time unless I could find a "mission" to justify my return. Nerayo assured me that, for someone with my background, there was always a lot to do, and he could guarantee that they would find me a mission. And then, just as I was about to get on the last truck leaving the base camp, he thanked me for having made this long and arduous trip to the field. He had *thanked* me—and I was deeply touched by his generosity.

Quickly, albeit reluctantly, I climbed into the truck that would take me back to a hot bath, digestible food, and a real bed while these courageous people would continue to live in the bush and face death every day until they had regained their independence or were crushed.

We never reached Port Sudan that night. The driver estimated that we would probably run out of fuel long before we could get there, so we stopped at a small EPLF supply depot just inside the Eritrean border. The depot was next door to a large, outdoor prisoner-of-war camp that contained at least three hundred Ethiopian soldiers, all in loincloths and the ubiquitous plastic sandals that were an EPLF gift for every POW. Most of them were illiterate Oromo boys who had been press-ganged into the army and sent to the front as cannon fodder, many without weapons, ammunition, or even basic military training. Although these prisoners were scattered over a flat field, the two EPLF guards assigned to them sat at the edge of the field, obviously bored, with their Kalashnikovs leaning against a tree. They weren't in the least concerned that their prisoners might try to escape and go home because they knew that any Ethiopian soldiers who returned to the front lines would be summarily shot as cowards, spies, or traitors. Instead, the guards and the prisoners slept or smoked or played cards together.

A few minutes after we arrived at the depot, the young combatant in charge of the station, nicknamed "Teacher," greeted me with open arms, smiled enigmatically, and told me to sit on the stairs in front of the house so that he could wash my feet before bringing me tea and food. I thought he was making an ironic joke about a black man washing the feet of a white man, but he was serious. He soon returned with a basin of water, some soap, and a towel, explaining that it is an Eritrean tradition to wash the feet of weary travelers who have come a long way. The honor of such a ceremony was a little embarrassing, but once I relaxed, I enjoyed it immensely.

Over the next few days, nothing seemed to happen. Because of a serious fuel shortage, no cars or trucks passed in either direction, although this was the most important road between Orotta and Port Sudan and there was, in effect, no communication with the outside. Every night I stayed awake listening for the truck grinding its gears up the steep grades that would take me back to Port Sudan and home, but all I heard were the wild dogs howling for their mates. During the day, I wandered aimlessly in the open space of the small depot, feeling caged and thinking that somebody must have made a mistake. I stomped around impatiently, complaining because I couldn't get word to my wife that I was fine. Eventually Teacher, who couldn't have been more than half my age, sat me down and quietly but emphatically told me that he hadn't seen his wife for more than five years and didn't even know whether she was still alive. That was all he said, but I had heard and been properly chastised and educated.

When I had finally fallen asleep on the third day, one of the men who worked at the station frantically shook me and told me in broken but coherent English that there was a woman outside who urgently needed help for her child. The boy was burning up with fever, shivered uncontrollably, and intermittently had massive seizures. We all knew the boy would surely die very soon from cerebral malaria unless we could bring his fever down, but in this out-of-the way station, there was no refrigerator, no ice, and no aspirin. For the next hour we took turns wrapping the child in a wet mattress cover, but the convulsions continued, each one driving the mother closer to the edge of despair. After one particularly violent convulsion, the boy just sighed and gently stopped breathing as we stood by in a rage of helplessness. The mother just stood there frozen, not making a sound until she realized that her child had just died. Then she gave one long howl of agony, picked up her dead child, and shuffled back into the darkness from whence she had come, sobbing silently.

Two nights later, another old truck that had found some stored fuel came wheezing up the steep roads. The Swiss ENT (ear, nose, and throat) surgeon who had been training the first prospective Eritrean ENT surgeon was standing in the open back of the truck. The threat of another major Ethiopian offensive had fizzled out, and there was now enough fuel to get us back to Port Sudan. After just a week in Eritrea, I felt liberated but sad.

Note

1 Johanna Fleischhauer, *Von Krieg betroffene Kinder* (Opladen, Germany, and Farmington Hills, Mich.: Budrich UniPress, 2008).

· 6 ·

SOLOMUNA

The name "Solomuna" had come up in passing several times during our discussions about the social problems facing innocent children who were caught up in a ferocious war. But when I asked what Solomuna was, the fighters assured me that I wouldn't be interested. When, on my return a year later, the name came up in a very different context, I asked again, and Assefaw explained that it was the main orphanage in the base camp. Because the development of children growing up under conditions of extreme deprivation was an issue of abiding interest for me, Nerayo had indeed found me a mission to justify my return: assessing how the orphanage was being managed, evaluating its social structure, and determining how this harsh terrain and dangerous social environment were affecting the physical and emotional health of these profoundly deprived children. So Assefaw offered to take me to Solomuna.

After we had wound our way through dry riverbeds and around huge boulders, Assefaw announced that we had arrived in Solomuna. But to an inexperienced eye like mine, there was no sign of habitation and nothing to see except endless sand flats stretching to the horizon in all directions, dotted here and there by an occasional thornbush. The only noise that disturbed the tomblike silence was the gentle hissing sound of the sand as it was being driven by the hot winds and the sad song of the mourning doves. I found it incomprehensible that this was Solomuna—a safe haven for three hundred orphans. Where were the children? Where did they sleep and eat and play? Where could they possibly hide in case of an air raid alarm?

Then, a slender young man surfaced like an apparition from behind the dunes, welcomed us, and gave Assefaw a warm hug. That man was Yemane Dawit, formerly in charge of hospital administration and now the head of the Authority of Social Affairs (ASA). Yemane was in charge of all the civilian social welfare programs in the base camps, including Solomuna.

Snapshot: Yemane Dawit

It was hard to imagine that this gentle, self-effacing man had spent the last fourteen years—his entire adult life—fighting the Ethiopian juggernaut. In time, I would discover that there was nothing special about Yemane's presence. After decades of confronting death, almost all of the combatants had overcome not only their fears but also their hatred of the enemy, even when circumstances forced them to kill. Was it possible that fourteen years of living with death and dying had turned Yemane and his comrades into soft-spoken, painfully modest, but fierce combatants?

After graduating from high school in Asmara, Yemane had enrolled in Haile Selassie University in Addis Ababa for an advanced degree in public administration. Despite decades of political tensions between Ethiopia and Eritrea, the emperor supported the brightest academically qualified Eritrean students with full scholarships for advanced degrees in medicine, engineering, public administration, sociology, and other career paths. These Eritrean graduate students spent their days studying diligently for a graduate degree and their nights debating radical texts and plotting how to evict the Ethiopian occupation army from their country.

Like many of his Eritrean classmates, Yemane was about to be arrested by the Ethiopian police for his subversive activities, so he fled to Eritrea, where he joined one of the earliest military formations of the independence movement. His first major assignment in the EPLF was to organize a frontline field hospital for combat casualties and secure drugs and other medical supplies on the black market. Although a graduate student in public administration, he also performed minor surgical procedures by himself and assisted the trained surgeons in major operations.

As the casualties mounted, the hospital had to be repeatedly enlarged from a frontline hospital to a tertiary care hospital. In 1978, the EPLF, on the brink of victory, was suddenly overrun by massive Soviet tanks and MIG jet fighters and forced to retreat. Adopting a strategy that the Chinese Red Army had often used successfully and that the EPLF cadre had studied in detail, the combatants retreated to the mountains of Sahel Province, where even advanced Soviet tanks couldn't penetrate. The entire hospital, including patients, beds, mattresses, X-ray equipment, surgical instruments, and supplies, had to be evacuated in a hurry, but there weren't enough trucks, cars, and ambulances to transport more than the most severely injured combatants, who would surely die if left behind.

Wounded combatants, including those who could barely walk themselves, carried those who couldn't walk at all. After ten grueling days of hiding from Ethiopian MIGs during the day and stumbling over the rocky terrain at night, with barely enough food or water to survive, they finally reached the protected valleys of the Northern Highlands. Under Yemane's direction, the Central Hospital was reassembled. The surgical, medical, orthopedic, and obstetrical wards, operating theaters, a pharmacy, a clinical laboratory, and whatever else belongs to a tertiary care hospital were now distributed over four kilometers along a meandering dry riverbed, dubbed the "longest hospital in the world."

For some reason that I didn't understand, Yemane had been switched from his position as hospital administrator to head the ASA. He was now in charge of all the civilian social welfare programs in the liberated zone, including the Solomuna orphanage.

While we were sipping the traditional glass of spiced tea in a sheltered spot in the bush, Assefaw explained to Yemane that I had a special interest in the alternative developmental pathways available to children who grow up under conditions of extreme adversity. What I was after apparently made sense to Yemane, who suggested that we go on a tour of the Solomuna orphanage so that I could see for myself.

The moment we crossed into the center of the orphanage compound, our entrance triggered pandemonium: a horde of at least fifty children, all under seven years of age, descended on us like angry hornets whose nest had been disturbed. They clawed, scratched, punched, or bit their way through the crowd until they got close enough to get a firm hold on a piece of clothing, an arm, or even a leg and then held on for dear life. In their demands for affection and physical contact, it didn't matter whether the people they latched onto were white or black, male or female, Eritrean or non-Eritrean. Wave after wave of these aggressive children assaulted us, demanding to be picked up and burying themselves against our bodies as if they wanted to be assimilated, while they deliberately ignored the counselors who fed, washed, and comforted them every day. What were they looking for so desperately that only strangers could satisfy?

The orphanage had originally been located in Keren, one of the largest towns in Eritrea. During a major Ethiopian offensive, the orphans had been evacuated to Solomuna, deep in the rugged mountains of Sahel Province. But they paid a heavy price for their physical safety: the place was too cold in the winter and too hot in the summer—even by Eritrean standards.

Most of the children slept in large canvas tents that were pitched on flat terrain next to the dry riverbed. Although the drought had by now lasted for more than four years, there were occasional cloudbursts when the rain poured down the parched cliffs in torrents, sending flashfloods down the riverbeds and washing away everything, including the tents. For their protection during the big rains, many children were moved to a large cave that was so well camouflaged that it couldn't be seen from the outside. Inside, it looked like a long hall along which about thirty or forty children slept side by side, tightly packed together. At an elevation of six thousand feet, the crowding probably kept them warm, but it also prevented them from turning from one side to the other without disturbing their neighbors.

Here in Solomuna, about eighty counselors were responsible for the health, safety, and development of the three hundred orphans, who ranged in age from three to seven. This was a heavy responsibility, since their daily schedules allowed the counselors barely enough time to complete all of their physical chores. Still, at least in principle, a ratio of four children to one counselor should have left enough time for counselors to give the children the affection they craved, to comfort them when they were sad or afraid, and to play with them when they wanted to play. Perhaps undiplomatically, I asked Yemane whether there might not be some way in which counselors could set aside a little more time each day to provide the children with the emotional care and social and intellectual stimulation needed to facilitate their healthy development.

Yemane agreed that Solomuna was badly understaffed and that the counselors had been overworked ever since the orphanage was first founded in Keren. But in this inhospitable, dangerous environment, the counselors' first concern was to make sure that the children were safe, stayed physically healthy and clean, and got enough to eat. To support this explanation, Yemane read me an informal list of all the chores that each counselor had to carry out every day to meet these demands. The list seemed endless.

Most of the counselors were young women who had joined the EPLF to fight the Ethiopian invaders, and they were probably not prepared to look after very unhappy orphaned children. Instead of being able to join their comrades in the trenches, they had to prepare enough food for three hundred children at least twice a day and make sure that every child got enough to eat but didn't horde food, steal food from others, or go on a hunger strike. They also had to collect firewood in the barren, deforested hills. And they had to carry enough water from long distances to cook and to wash not only the children but also their clothes, as the occasional dust storms left the children so dirty that they sometimes had to be washed twice in the same day.

Many of the children were afraid of the dark when they first came to Solomuna, so the ASA established a policy whereby at least one counselor would sleep in the same tent with the children every night and be available in case one woke up in a panic and needed some comfort and reassurance. As an elaboration of that policy, the counselors were rotated through all the dormitories on a monthly basis so that, given enough time, they would one day know the names of all the children. For similar reasons, the children were assigned to their quarters—whether tent, dormitory, or cave—according to chronological age, presumably to facilitate peer-group formation.

In the daytime, the orphans under age six had to stay together in the central area of the orphanage campus so that the counselors could make sure they didn't wander off into the hills and get taken by wild animals. The youngest children had to stay close to the center of the campus so they could be shepherded into an underground shelter as soon as an air raid alarm sounded. As a result, they had almost nothing to do all day except to sit in the middle of the campus and stare into space, throw rocks at each other, or play with plastic toys that good-hearted Europeans had sent them but that usually broke in less than an hour.

The older children followed a different routine. Immediately after breakfast, they scattered into the surrounding hills until they found a shady spot among the rocks, where they spent the whole day climbing like goats, joking, teasing, and fighting, until it was safe for them to come down for their evening meal. After supper, they then had a free evening to hunt for rabbits, field mice, and snakes, or else they amused themselves by tyrannizing the younger children.

Tents, beds, mattresses, and blankets were always in short supply and in great demand; two, three, or sometimes even four children often had to share one mattress. Given the high density of vulnerable children in the tents, diarrhea, upper respiratory infections, and other childhood diseases sometimes spread uncontrolled.

There were rumors that a poliomyelitis epidemic was spreading in other parts of the country, and everyone was waiting anxiously for disaster to strike Solomuna next. On several occasions, the Medical Department had tried to establish a cold chain to bring vaccines across the hot sands from Port Sudan by equipping camels with battery-powered refrigerators, but often the vaccines either never even reached Port Sudan or were spoiled by the time they reached the hospital.

The tour had given me a good idea about the desperate physical and psychological condition of the children and the enormous problems facing the ASA staff who cared for them, as well as an entirely different perspective on the effects of war on vulnerable children. When, after the tour, Yemane asked me to give the staff some suggestions as to how they could improve the quality of life for these children, I was at a loss. Up to this point I had spent all of three hours walking through the institution and seeing what I could learn from observing the children's behavior. How could I possibly advise the counselors who were at home in this culture, knew the language, and had by now spent many years looking after the children? Still, I owed them feedback based on what I had learned from my own studies of children raised in entirely different social contexts and physical environments, so I agreed to try my best with the proviso that my comments would probably be more helpful after I had digested whatever I had seen and heard up to this point. Yemane agreed and invited me to spend a few days at the orphanage to get better acquainted with the place, its physical setting, and the social context. We agreed to make no concrete plans until Iba ("Father"), the director of the orphanage, and several of his key staff members could join us the next day.

After breakfast the next morning, Yemane called together the senior staff to discuss what could and should be done to improve the lot of the orphans. Iba began by summarizing the measures that had already been tried but with little or no success. I suggested that it might be more productive to first get some idea of the magnitude of the problem: how many orphans were suffering from treatable medical conditions? How many had psychosocial problems that required attention? What was the nature of those problems? What human and material resources were available in the orphanage that could be appropriated for their welfare? Only when we had answers to these questions could we try to tailor feasible remedies.

Such checklists are routinely used in Western clinical settings as screening devices, but there was obviously no such thing for Eritrean children in the base camps or, for that matter, in Eritrea—period! Since it seemed to me that such a list might be useful as a point of departure, I tried to reconstruct one from memory, doing my best to make the individual items as straightforward and locally relevant as possible so that the counselors could utilize the checklist with minimal need for additional training.

Two senior counselors who were fluent in Tigrinya and English reviewed my list and pruned out several items that made no sense in the base camps. Ultimately, we ended up with twenty-one items that were behavioral indicators of emotional problems as well as an inventory of serious organic illnesses. These became the basis of a questionnaire we used to assess the Solomuna orphans. After several unavoidable delays, we managed to prepare a comprehensive report detailing our findings, which the ASA reviewed and approved.[1]

The group we interviewed consisted of sixty-eight girls and fifty-one boys, with a mean age of 5.1 (range 3.4–7.2) years, who had all lived in the orphanage for at least two years. According to the counselors' best available information, most of the children had been present when their parents either were killed by enemy soldiers or died from chronic illnesses, and they had no known extended family members who could have taken them in and given them a home.

In addition to their delayed growth patterns, more than half of the orphans had active malaria, forty suffered from chronic upper respiratory infections, sixteen had active tuberculosis, and ten were suffering from scurvy. Most had at least two or more serious medical conditions, and as far as the nurse who occasionally visited the orphanage could estimate, of all the children whose checklists were examined, only seven were judged to be symptom free and healthy by local criteria.

The prevalence of emotional and psychological signs and symptoms of distress was even more alarming. More than three-quarters of the children had frequent sleep disturbance (night terrors, sleep walking, insomnia, excessive sleeping); nearly two-thirds had clinically significant eating disorders (overeating, refusing to eat, hoarding, pica); and more than half either made excessive demands on the counselors or deliberately avoided all human contact. More than half were mildly to moderately depressed; others were overly aggressive (by Eritrean standards). At least eleven were significantly delayed in speech and language acquisition; and while no one felt competent to make more than an informed guess about the prevalence of language disorders, that number was probably much greater because many of the children had been close to cannon fire and other explosions.

The Eritrean Relief Association, by all accounts the most effective relief organization in all of East Africa, regularly brought the children supplementary protein feedings. At the same time, combatants working in the rear areas raised chickens, collected eggs, and grew vegetables on their small plots of sandy soil; these they distributed equally among the orphans and the severely wounded fighters. The orphans therefore received the most nutritious diets available anywhere in the base camps. Yet they failed to develop along normal developmental lines.

To determine why the best-fed orphans failed to show normal growth curves, Dr. Elizabeth Jareg, a child psychiatrist from the Swedish Save the Children Organization, compared the monthly weight and growth charts of the orphans with those of a comparable group of children in a nearby refugee camp living with at least one surviving parent. These refugee children had been subjected to many of the same deprivations and hardships as the Solomuna orphans, but had not received any supplementary feedings. According to Dr. Jareg's findings, most of the orphans gained weight normally during the first few months after arriving in Solomuna but then either stopped gaining or actually lost weight. By contrast, the nearby refugee children continued to show normally sustained developmental growth and weight patterns. She concluded that the orphans were probably suffering from "non-organic failure to thrive"; in other words, their severe emotional deprivation led to undernutrition. She predicted that no amount of supplementary feedings would restore them to a normal growth pattern unless they received more personal attention, emotional support, and social stimulation—all at the same time.[2]

Almost nothing was known about the clinical history of these children that would explain why some of the orphans who had been so severely affected showed almost no improvement over time while others seemed to recover quickly once they had adapted to life in the Solomuna orphanage. The best that the counselors could do with the available records was to reconstruct what must or might have happened to bring the orphans to Solomuna.

Snapshot: Barentu

Barentu is the name of an Eritrean town where the EPLF and the Ethiopian army had fought a tank battle of historic proportions. After the Ethiopians withdrew from the town, EPLF scouts discovered a four-year-old girl wandering aimlessly in the ruins. She knew that her first name was Ghidei, a very popular name in Eritrea, but for some reason she didn't know her family name (patronymic) or the name of her village of origin. From an Eritrean perspective, she had therefore lost her identity and, in effect, was nobody. At a loss as to what else they could do, the combatants took turns carrying her on their backs on the long trek through the contested area until they had brought her to Solomuna.

There she tried to fit into the daily routines, but ruminated constantly about having lost her identity. She badgered everyone who would listen, asking if they had any news about her family, even though she didn't know the family name. When the other children made fun of her, she ran away and sometimes was gone for several days before returning to the orphanage. The counselors were convinced that she was so deeply ashamed of being a nonperson that she couldn't bear to be with children who knew who they were. To give her some kind of identity, the counselors gave her the name Barentu, after the town where she had been lost and found, but that only made matters worse. Like every else, she knew that no one else in all of Eritrea had ever been called "Barentu." To erase that mistake and give her the sense of belonging to an extended family, Yemane Dawit offered to give her his patronymic. But by then it was too late: the name Barentu had stuck, and no one ever called her Dawit.

After the war, most of the orphans who had not yet been reunited with their extended families were transferred to a large urban orphanage, where families from all parts of the country came to search for their missing relatives. But no one ever came to claim Barentu. Ghidei-Barentu-Dawit had lost her identity.

Snapshot: "Salman" or "Eyasu"

The experience of a child whose identity was torn apart by ethnic and religious conflicts gave us at least an inkling of just how difficult it was to find the right home for a child whose past had been wiped out. Shortly before the decisive tank battle at Afabet that would seal the defeat of the Ethiopian armed forces, the women of Afabet (the population of which is 90 percent Muslim) had been warned about the ensuing battle and urged by the EPLF to evacuate the town as quickly as possible. Everyone who was even marginally mobile scrambled for a seat in a truck or on the back of a camel to get out of harm's way. In the confusion, one young boy, who had been raised in the Orthodox (Coptic) tradition, was inadvertently left behind. He survived the tank battle unharmed, but no one knew who he was neither his patronymic nor his village of origin. After the smoke settled, he began to search everywhere for his mother, but the quest was pointless: she had left on a truck going to one of five different refugee camps, but no one knew which one.

Since the boy had no relatives who could look after him, he was temporarily placed in one of the group homes that had room for two more children. Like most Muslim families in Eritrea, the family that had heard about the boy's arrival was strongly opposed to placing any unaccompanied child of unknown religious background into any institutional setting, especially when the majority of children in that group home were Coptic Christians. The Muslim family that had stayed behind now gave him a Muslim name, Salman. He adjusted well to his new family, participated in all the Mohammedan prayers and other rituals, had an outstanding academic record in a local Muslim school, and seemed to be fully integrated in the Muslim culture. But that was by no means the end of the odyssey.

After searching for her son in refugee camps and local towns for eight long years, the boy's birth mother learned about a possible place where her son was living. Eventually she found a boy of about the same age and was convinced that it was indeed her son, even though she had last seen him when he was only three. She wanted to take him back to a Christian environment, but the Muslim family that had been raising the boy in the Muslim tradition for the past eight years refused to give him up. The Ministry of Labour and Human Welfare (as the ASA would later be called) still had legal custody of the boy, but in its efforts to reach a solution that would be fair to both sides, it finally decided that the boy should be returned to his biological mother. The boy was given a new name, Eyasu, and a new patronymic; was accepted by the village where his mother lived; and received religious instructions in the teachings of the Coptic Church. Follow-up studies indicated that it took him at least four years to recover something resembling a sense of identity and be reintegrated into the community of his choice.

The survey gave me a rough idea about the most urgent social needs that, if fulfilled, would probably make the lives of the orphans more stimulating and safe. There were also some very simple maneuvers whereby the staff might improve the children's emotional well-being.

For example, the policy of having at least one counselor sleep with the children every night had certainly been an important step forward in the social reintegration of the orphans. Presumably, it gave them a feeling of security and reassured them that they were not alone in this cruel world. On the other hand, rotating the counselors from tent to tent on a monthly basis might very well have had the opposite effect of showing the children that adults were not to be trusted. Having barely begun to rely on and trust one caregiver, they would have to start all over again in building a feeling of trust thirty days later—an effort that must have been especially difficult for orphans whose parents had disappeared unpredictably but permanently. Furthermore, it seemed that no single counselor would ever get to know all of the children, and even if one did, what benefit would it bring?

Moreover, as far as I knew, there was no evidence that children of the same age are more likely to form stable peer groups than children of different ages within a reasonable age range. On the other hand, there is some anecdotal evidence that when children of different ages live together as a group, the older children learn to look out for their younger "siblings" and, in the process, naturally learn how to care for each other.

Therefore, I suggested that, instead of every counselor being rotated through all the dormitories each month, one reliable and experienced counselor should be appointed as a permanent houseparent for all the children in each dormitory. If possible, an assistant houseparent should also be recruited to share the workload during the day. And having a permanent housemother looking after children of different ages would amount to an almost natural extended family rather than an institutional collective.

To give the children the sense that their dormitories were also their homes, I also suggested that they be encouraged to help decorate their quarters; perhaps the possibility of hanging favorite pictures (but not propaganda posters) in their dormitories was a foreign idea, but it was still an idea worth pursuing. In addition, the children should have designated places where they could keep their personal belongings. Further, all children should be expected to participate in daily household chores, in keeping the house and surrounding grounds clean, in cultivating small vegetable gardens, and in growing trees and the like.

I also suggested that regular workshops be held on normal and deviant child development, the special needs of traumatized children, and strategies for promoting cooperation and self-reliance. These workshops should be open to all staff members, regardless of whether they were directly involved in the care of the children. Whenever necessary, the workshops should also provide the children with an opportunity to participate in the discussions that affected their daily lives.

Yemane estimated that if these changes in the organization of the orphanage had an effect, it would take at least a year before we could expect to see any significant improvement in the emotional well-being of the children (and perhaps also the staff). Therefore, I planned to return to Solomuna in twelve to eighteen months and participate in assessing what effect, if any, the social transformation of the orphanage might have had on the orphans.

Notes

1 The findings from these interviews have been published in detail elsewhere and are here only summarized. See Peter H. Wolff et al., "The Orphans of Eritrea: A Comparison Study," *Journal of Child Psychology and Child Psychiatry* 36, no. 4 (1995): 633–644.
2 Elizabeth Jareg, Report *of Consultancy Visit to Eritrea* (Oslo, Norway: Redd Barna, 1988).

· 7 ·

SOLOMUNA REVISITED

By 1988, most of Eritrea except the urban centers was under EPLF control. Therefore, it was a good time to visit Solomuna to see how the orphans were faring and what effect, if any, the social reorganization of the orphanage had had on their physical and psychological development. After the customary glass of tea, Yemane and I made another tour through the orphanage. I sensed that the social atmosphere had changed to some extent, but I couldn't pinpoint exactly what was different.

The moment we crossed over into the children's playground, it became obvious that the orphans still had a long way to go before we could say with any confidence that they were on the way to recovery. The moment they saw us coming—and they seemed to be on constant alert for something interesting or frightening—the new group of three- to seven-year-olds came running. These children had spent almost two years in what we hoped would be a therapeutic community of child-care counselors, yet, like those I had met on my first visit, these children also pushed themselves through the crowd to get to us, secured a hold onto a hand or leg or a piece of clothing, and held on for dear life. However, their attack on us seemed far less ferocious than the one we had experienced eighteen months before.

The counselors were now able to control the children with a few firm words instead of physical cuffing or ear pulling. An even more encouraging sign was that when we, as strangers, didn't give them the attention they demanded, the frustrated children turned for affection and comfort to the counselors whom they had totally shunned eighteen months earlier. While it was far from obvious what this switch in their behavior might mean for their long-range recovery, it seemed to me that turning to their counselors for solace was an important step forward in their eventual social reintegration.

There were also a few objective indicators that the children might be on the mend. While reorganizing the social environment of the orphanage had probably had an important overall effect on the physical and psychological well-being of the orphans, environmental factors also probably played key roles in their improvement.

For example, the poorly ventilated tents in which the orphans lived were too hot in the summer and much too cold in the winter. So a group of orphans from the Zero School, many of whom had spent their early years in Solomuna, gave up their summer vacations and, in collaboration with their teachers, who had also forgone their vacations, set about building houses out of slabs of stone and slate harvested from the surrounding hills. Stone houses would be cooler in the summer and might be warmer in the winter; more importantly, they would withstand the onslaught of the flash floods and make no additional demands on limited resources because there was no shortage of building materials. Such houses were already widely distributed throughout the base camps of Sahel Province. With sufficient flat terrain on which to build them, enough stone houses could be built to ensure that no more than twenty-five children had to sleep in one dormitory. Iba and Yemane had somehow managed to requisition enough additional beds and mattresses so that no more than three children ever had to share one mattress—a luxury that also probably reduced the "ping-pong" transmission of communicable diseases from bed to bed.

Well-qualified women who had raised their own children had been recruited from the nearby refugee camp to be permanent housemothers, and enough women were recruited to ensure that there was now at least one housemother for each dormitory. Most of the mothers had immediately understood what their role as housemother should be and quickly created the culturally sensitive supportive emotional atmosphere of an extended family. The few who had volunteered for the salary, which was miniscule, didn't work out well and were eventually dismissed.

Moreover, each stone house was now home to children of mixed ages. The gangs that had once bullied the younger children had dissolved, and the constant bickering that had previously made organized games and cooperative play impossible had greatly diminished. The more adventurous and self-confident children were encouraged to organize their own expeditions into the surrounding hills to hunt for mice, snakes and berries.

The teachers noticed that the children seemed to be learning faster from each other than from their teachers. When the older ones came home after spending several hours in kindergarten, they seemed eager to share what they had learned with the younger ones. That, in turn, stimulated the younger ones to ask questions that had never occurred to the older ones and that the older ones couldn't answer. Sometimes they then went back to their teachers for clarification. In this way, all the children discovered that it is much better to learn by asking questions than by memorizing arbitrary facts. From her extensive experience in teaching European preschool children, Maria Montessori had come to the same conclusion in a very different culture: "When younger and older children work alongside each other, peer teaching is common. The older children who are settled in the environment enjoy helping out the younger ones who, for example, want to know how to work with an apparatus that the older ones are familiar with. There is nothing that makes (one) learn more than teaching it to someone else."[1]

Other evidence of improved well-being was evident in the results of a more detailed version of the same symptom checklist we had used to assess the children eighteen months earlier. The counselors now reported far fewer children showing signs of sleep disturbances, far fewer eating disturbances, 40–45 percent fewer signs of developmental language delays, and 40 percent fewer symptoms of disturbed social interactions with adults or peers

Additionally, the nurse who regularly visited the orphanage to check on the health of the children reported that there had been no change in the children's diet over the past two years, yet those who had spent those years in Solomuna not only had far fewer symptoms or signs of physical disorder than the original sample of Solomuna orphans, but were also in a far better nutritional state. Almost none of them had any signs or symptoms of being undernourished. The results were consistent with Dr. Jareg's observation that the orphans in the first sample had been suffering from nonorganic failure to thrive and that social interventions—even the most basic—would be as essential for recovery and development of the orphans as an excellent diet. In short, most of the recommendations made after my first visit had been implemented or refined and improved. Over that time, sleeping disorders, eating disorders, language delays, and impaired social interactions with adults and children had been reduced by half in almost all cases.[2]

And there was still another improvement in their social atmosphere—one that could not have been anticipated. When the Union of Eritrean Truck Drivers, who worked in Khartoum, heard about the plight of the Solomuna orphans, they promptly tithed themselves to buy a large electricity generator and two electric washing machines to do the laundry and give the counselors more hours every day to tend to the children's emotional and social needs. Now that the orphanage had electricity, the generators were also turned on once a week for movie night. The children, their caregivers, combatants, sometimes whole families—in fact, everyone who had free time—gathered around a huge boulder where someone had mounted a film screen to watch whatever movies could be imported on loan from Sudan or brought into the camps by returning combatants. The program of movies, largely chosen by the ASA, included cartoons, children's stories, and feature films, and showed a strong bias toward documentaries. For the first time in their lives, the orphans were exposed to an entirely new world on the other side of the mountains.

The combined efforts of the ASA and the community at large had gone a long way toward enhancing the quality of life for these Solomuna orphans. However, it remained to be seen whether these changes had a significant impact—direct or indirect—on their psychological development, emotional state, and social integration.

Notes

1 Maria Montessori, The *Child, Society and the World: Unpublished Speeches and Writings* (Oxford, UK: Clio Press, 1989).
2 Peter H. Wolff and Gebremeskel Fesseha, "The Orphans of Eritrea: A Five-Year Follow-Up Study," *Journal of Child Psychology and Psychiatry* 40, no. 8 (1999): 1231–1237; see also Peter H. Wolff and Gebremeskel Fesseha, "The Orphans of Eritrea: Are Orphanages Part of the Problem or Part of the Solution?" *American Journal of Psychiatry* 155, no. 10 (1998): 1319–1324.

· 8 ·

CENTERS FOR MOTHERS AND INFANTS

Shortly after the EPLF had split from the ELF in 1970, it proclaimed that all heterosexual activity among combatants would henceforth be strictly forbidden and punishable by six months of hard labor, while overt homosexual activities would be punishable by execution—although the death sentence had probably never been carried out. The leadership justified these extreme prohibitions against sexual freedom on the grounds that any sort of sexual activity under the crowded living conditions would inevitably undermine morale, lead to jealousy, and weaken the fighting spirit of combatants, whereas sexual abstinence would strengthen their fighting spirit.

However, political rectitude was no match for human nature. It could hardly have come as a surprise to the leadership that when young men and women live, fight, and die together in the trenches, it is probably inevitable that female combatants will become pregnant and have to decide whether to carry their pregnancies to term or abort the fetus. Those who carried their pregnancies to term and returned to the front would constantly worry about their babies and about who was looking after their welfare, and, as folk wisdom has it, such worries weaken the fighting spirit.

After the First EPLF Congress in 1977, the leadership relaxed its policies on sex. Contraceptives were made available to the combatants, who, after some time, were able to petition their commanders for permission to marry. As sexual sanctions loosened, increasing numbers of female combatants, who now made up a third of all the fighting forces, became pregnant and had to make the difficult choice to either terminate the pregnancy, carry the fetus to term and then leave the baby to return to the front lines, or have the baby and remain behind to care for it. Those who chose to remain behind and care for their babies felt guilty about deserting their comrades; those who chose to give birth and then quickly return to the front lines felt guilty about abandoning their babies to someone else's care.

One evening, while we were having supper in the orphanage compound and chatting in English (to include me), a young woman in military fatigues appeared out of the dark carrying her Kalashnikov in one arm and a two-week-old infant in the other. She looked sullen and depressed, refused the invitation to join the group, and sat down alone in a dark corner. There she leaned her Kalashnikov against a wall, covered her baby's face with a gauze cloth, and proceeded to feed it.

I thought the gauze cover was a hygienic measure to protect the baby from harmful germs, but one of the counselors explained that its purpose was to prevent the baby from seeing its mother's face while she was feeding it. From some radio broadcast, perhaps the "BBC Focus on Africa," they had heard that eye-to-eye contact is a powerful evolutionary mechanism for establishing a strong emotional bond between mother and infant, so many of the young women who had given birth in the field but expected to return to the front lines as soon as possible covered their babies' faces before each feeding to spare their children the agony of breaking the mother-infant bond. They also avoided sleeping in the same room with their babies and kept all forms of social communication with them to a minimum.

So that pregnant combatants wouldn't have to choose between having an abortion so that they could return to the front or abandoning their comrades to care for their infants in the rear-area camps, the Medical Department, with Assefaw's support, joined forces with the ASA under the guidance of Gebremeskel Fesseha, whom we called Gere, to build and staff a center for mothers and babies where the women could devote themselves full-time to the care of their infants for the first six months and then stay with their infants while taking up some EPLF responsibilities that could be carried out in the rear areas.

Snapshot: Gere

Gebremeskel Fesseha, or Gere, on staff at the ASA, was responsible for all childhood-related research activities in the base camps. The younger son of a very poor farming family, he had been raised in a small village of the Central Highlands. After completing his high school education in Eritrea, he enrolled at Haile Selassie University in Addis Ababa, where he studied sociology and social work.

Most of the Eritrean university students who were studying abroad had the reputation, whether deserved or not, of being political troublemakers and, like them, Gere was constantly in danger of being arrested by the Ethiopian authorities. To avoid arrest, he left the university but stayed in Addis Ababa and took a position as assistant pharmacist, turning an economically failing drugstore into a profitable business. Eventually, life in the capital became unbearable for Eritreans, and Gere took a managerial position in a weaving factory in one of the provinces, where he reorganized the labor force and turned it into a thriving cooperative based on a profit-sharing plan for all employees. By 1974, life in Ethiopia had become so oppressive that he left the country and joined the EPLF.

His first assignment was to screen all volunteers, assess their motives for joining the Front, and weed out all potential spies, deserters, and psychologically unstable volunteers. He was also responsible for assessing how the EPLF could best make use of the special skills and talents of each potential combatant. As one of very few academically trained social workers in the base camps, Gere became a key player in all of the ASA's research activities. Without his patience, his generosity, and his expert knowledge of child development in an Eritrean context, most of our studies could not have been completed. Whenever any foreign visitors or any NGO from abroad needed help with some project involving children, women, refugee families, and so on, the routine response was "Go ask Gere."

And that is exactly what I did whenever I needed his guidance on how to proceed.

By 1984, seven of the larger military and service units in the liberated zones, including the Central Hospital in Orotta, the Zero School, and the Logistics and Security Departments, had all established centers for mothers and their infants like those described above. Maternity leave was extended to two or three years, and day-care cooperatives were established where mothers could alternate between caring for groups of infants or toddlers and carrying on with their duties in the rear areas. Workshops for both men and women were organized to educate the combatants about the importance of close personal bonds between parents and children even during the early months after birth.

· 9 ·

THE ZERO SCHOOL

In 1988, when I made my third visit to the base camps, Assefaw suggested that this might be a good time for me to visit the Zero School so that I could see for myself how the EPLF was educating the children and preparing them to participate in the rebuilding of their country after independence. The Zero School would, in time, turn out to be of critical importance to the success of the social revolution in Eritrea.

After bouncing up and down through an endless series of dry riverbeds, Assefaw stopped the car and announced that we had arrived at the Zero School—an underground facility for four to five thousand boys and girls aged seven to seventeen. I thought he must be joking. There was nothing to see except the endless dunes and sand flats surrounded in the distance by a ring of rugged red cliffs. It seemed incomprehensible to me that this lunar landscape could possibly be the campus of a boarding school—albeit an underground one.

After Assefaw had honked the car horn several times, a slender man with a finely chiseled face and high squeaky voice emerged like an apparition from behind the dunes and welcomed us. That man was Beraki Gebreselassie, a school teacher by profession, a committed combatant by conviction, and now head of the EPLF Education Department as well as a member of the EPLF Central Committee.

Once we each had a glass of spiced tea in our hands, Assefaw explained that I was particularly interested in the alternative pathways by which children learn under conditions of extreme adversity and are taught to question authority even when unquestioning obedience to programmed instructions would be far more convenient and cost-effective. With this introduction, Assefaw probably made it inevitable that Beraki and I would discover a common interest in the theory of intellectual development proposed by Jean Piaget, the highly respected Swiss developmental psychologist and philosopher of science, and in how that theory might be translated into a forward-looking pedagogy. Piaget had summarized his view on the goals of education succinctly:

Children should be able to do their own experimenting and their own research. Teachers, of course, can guide them by providing appropriate materials, but the essential thing is that in order for a child to understand something, he must construct it for himself, he must reinvent it. Every time we [try to] teach a child something, we keep him from reinventing it for himself. On the other hand, that which we allow him to discover by himself will remain with him visibly... for the rest of his life.[1]

In short, he started from the *a priori* assumption that action is the wellspring of all mental activity and, more specifically, of scientific thinking and knowing.

However, in Beraki's experience, the pursuit of knowledge for its own sake tends to spawn an intellectual elite that follows its own narrow academic interests and turns its back on the devastating consequences of poverty, ignorance, and superstition for society at large. And Piaget, in his analysis, had underestimated the importance of the social, economic, and cultural factors that shape the psychological development of children—those factors that especially serve as an educational framework for children growing up in underdeveloped countries. Beraki agreed that in affluent Western societies such as Switzerland, where nearly everyone belongs to the middle class and almost all children can read and write long before they enter elementary school, it might be possible to take the larger social-sociological context for granted and prepare children throughout primary and secondary school for the mastery of operational logic that need not have anything to do with their social surroundings; there, teachers can dedicate some of their precious teaching time to focusing exclusively on the process of intellectual development and the "having of wonderful ideas."[2] However, in poor countries like Eritrea, where over 90 percent of the population is illiterate, it would be a strategic and self-defeating mistake to educate a small minority of intellectuals who would occupy themselves with complex abstract problems that had nothing to do with the everyday burdens of the poor—those who must struggle every day to feed their families, their cattle, and themselves.

To counteract these tendencies, the Zero School research team was striving for a flexible curriculum that did not follow a preordained "lesson plan" of specific topics to be covered within a fixed timeframe; instead, they focused on the Socratic approach to learning through experimentation, discourse, and discovery. Beraki envisioned a curriculum based on the assumption that all children are naturally curious about the world around them and that their hunger for knowledge is insatiable until or unless their curiosity is squelched by the inanities of programmed instructions and reinforcement schedules. Thus, he considered the pedagogical methods of learning and teaching that followed logically from Piaget's theory of intellectual development to be particularly useful here at the Zero School because they were designed to encourage students to think independently and critically, to experiment in order to discover solutions rather than memorizing the naked facts that teachers dished out and that students were expected to regurgitate. A progressive approach to education of the kind implied by Piaget, as well as similar theories of cognitive development through action, could serve as a powerful shield against the internal enemies of a free society—namely, illiteracy, superstition, corruption, and a closed mind.

I might have objected that Beraki was perhaps drawing too sharp a line between practical and abstract knowing, since both paths eventually lead to the same goal. I might also have pointed out that Piaget had by no means been indifferent to the devastating effects that poverty can have on the intellectual development of young children. On the contrary, under the aegis of the United Nations Educational, Scientific and Cultural Organization (UNESCO), he had long agitated for the widespread use of preschool education to compensate the children of poor families for the lack of intellectual challenges offered them at home.

But the idea of sitting here in the middle of the desert with battle-hardened combatants who had fought a desperate thirty-year war for liberation and were now debating the finer points of theory and praxis—the extraction of theoretical meaning from practical action—as principles of pedagogy required such a remarkable power of imagination that it would merely have trivialized Beraki's essential point. As far as I know, what the Education Department was attempting to do here in the middle of the desert had never been tried elsewhere, at least not on a nationwide basis. Whether this goal was at all achievable or would eventually lead to too many internal contradictions remained to be seen, but at least the leadership of one small, insignificant country on the Horn of Africa was dedicated to trying.

So I kept quiet, convinced that it would be far more profitable to listen and learn than to squabble about technical details.

When it was time for Assefaw to return to the hospital, Beraki invited me to spend some days at the school so that I could see for myself how the students were learning, how the teachers were teaching, and how the students were learning by teaching. With a gentle smile, he suggested that we continue our conversation at another time and turned me over to one of the older students. This student brought me to a small cave dug into the side of one of the cliffs that was furnished with a real bed, a real mattress, and a small table. This would be my home for the next seven days.

Shortly after sunrise the next morning, I woke up to the happy laughter of children who were balancing on their backs huge containers of fresh water and bundles of firewood for breakfast while telling each other what must have been hilarious stories and jokes. Soon, a very pretty, shy girl knocked on my door, balancing a large tray with a bowl of water for washing, a small pot of spicy tea, warm rolls freshly baked in the school bakery, and a dish of Nerayo's precious strawberry jam. With great dignity and personal presence, she pointed at the tray and invited me in Tigrinya to enjoy my breakfast.

Promptly at seven in the morning, Ayn Alem Marcos—"Joe" for short—introduced himself and offered to be my guide and mentor for the next few days. He had taken a master's degree in education at an American university, spoke fluent English, had learned a great deal about educational systems in other countries, and was now in charge of all teacher training. After making sure that I had had enough breakfast, he invited me on a tour of the school, briefing me on the school's methods of operation and providing some concrete examples of how the school conceived of an Eritrean education for Eritrean children.

Origins and Operation

During the late 1970s, the EPLF established the first Zero School, so named because, at the time of its founding, it was virtually nothing but a primitive refuge for lost or abandoned orphans, refugee children, and children of combatants of various ages, most of whom had never been to school. There were no dormitories or school buildings, no desks or benches, no curriculum, no books, and almost no supplies for running a school. In other words, there was only a school with no resources, material or otherwise—a "zero" school.

The volunteers who would later become teachers had no experience in teaching; they had joined the EPLF to fight the Ethiopian invaders, not to look after and teach the next generation. And they certainly had no experience dealing with antisocial behavior, adolescent depression, withdrawal, and all the other signs and symptoms of emotional difficulties that are almost inevitable in any large boarding school for children and adolescents. But from the school's steady growth and the students' academic performance, they quickly learned that fighting in the front lines in no way limits the opportunities for studying, learning, and teaching.[3]

Over the next few years, under Beraki's direction, the Zero School expanded into a boarding school for more than two thousand orphans (including those from Solomuna), internal and external refugee children, and children of combatants, all from seven to eighteen years of age. By the end of the war, the student body had grown to five thousand. Depending on their elementary school background, age, and ability, they were taking courses in science, mathematics, geography, Eritrean history, Tigrinya, Tigre, Arabic, and English, as well as music, painting, sports, and handicrafts.

Formal classes were scheduled during the early morning hours from six to nine, before the Ethiopian MIGs began their daily search for human targets, and then again at dusk, after the planes had returned to base. Classes were held in camouflaged bunkers that had been gouged into the side of the mountain; in reinforced, brick-lined underground shelters; or anywhere else that students could study and learn without being disturbed by air raids. But there was never enough space in the makeshift facilities to accommodate all the students, nor were there enough benches, desks, and blackboards. To accommodate the overflow, classes were held under shade trees during the hours when the MIGs were probably back in their hangars. Two combatants always stood guard on the highest peaks surrounding the school and watched for incoming aircraft. As soon as they heard the familiar high-pitched screech, they fired shots from their Kalashnikovs to warn the students and teachers to find cover. Nevertheless, the MIGs still succeeded on several occasions in bombing the school and killing students.

To make up for a lack of blackboards, students and teachers improvised by creating erasable surfaces on which to write. At other times they sat together under the shade of a baobab tree, where they read to each other, wrote, discussed each other's essays, and searched for solutions to problems that inevitably arose in the course of their daily activities and could be used as exercises for integrating theory and practice. In the early evening, combatants and teachers sometimes joined the students to read by the flickering light of small, stinking kerosene lamps or a flashlight, even though flashlight batteries were very expensive.

By and large, students and teachers interacted as equals engaged in a common undertaking. They ate together, studied together, slept in the same cramped quarters, and worked together on communal projects that required a cooperative effort. They also competed as equals on team sports, with some of the students, combatants, and teachers becoming passionate soccer players. The only time in the whole day when the teachers were expected to, and did, exercise their authority as teachers was during scheduled classes; this was to ensure that they stayed on track so that the students could benefit from the subject matter under discussion. But even then, teachers and students respected each other as individuals, not as members of a social or economic class, and they addressed each other by first names; in this almost totally egalitarian society, there were no titles, no medals, and no uniforms. In short, they showed that it was possible to lay the foundations of a strong bond of friendship and solidarity that, according to much later reports, sustained the students long after they had completed their undergraduate education.

Governance

At the time of my visit to the Zero School, more than five thousand students were engaged in their studies and work projects. After seeing how smoothly the whole school functioned, I wondered how it was even possible for teachers committed to an egalitarian social environment to keep order in a classroom that was designed to encourage students to think critically, question authority, and, if necessary, directly confront authority.

Some of the more experienced teachers gave me some idea of how they had resolved the apparent contradiction without resorting to an authoritarian approach. Convinced that autonomy among the fighters had been a critical factor in maintaining their morale and discipline in the face of great danger, for example, Zero School administrators used the table of organization for Eritrea's combined fighting forces—the Eritrean People's Liberation Army

(EPLA), the armed wing of the EPLF—as their model and drafted an analogous table of organization for the school. Like the combatants, the students were divided into four main groups, each of which was under the "command" of an experienced combatant group leader who served as teacher. Each group was then divided into smaller groups, or "platoons," under the command of other experienced combatant group leaders. Each platoon, in turn, was divided into three or four groups of twenty to twenty-five students each. However, at this level of organization, the groups were supervised by and answerable to a student monitor who had been handpicked by the platoon leaders on the basis of demonstrated leadership skills. The youngest students were assigned to a special place in the table of organization because they had only recently left the orphanage.

Organizing the school's student body along quasi-military lines seemed to have had the desired effect of maintaining order without curtailing the egalitarian ethos or imposing a whole set of rules and regulations on the students in their daily routines. But the school's rules of conduct weren't always successful in restraining the older students.

Whenever the EPLA fought and won a major military victory, news quickly reached the students by the EPLF radio program, "Voice of the Masses." Stirred by patriotic fervor, some of the older students ran away to join the fighters and participate in the armed struggle. Those who managed to reach the front lines were immediately escorted back to the school, however, where they were firmly reminded that their responsibility for the time being was to study hard and learn as much as they could and that there would be ample opportunity for them to join the fighting after they had completed their schooling. But once the teachers realized that, for better or for worse, they wouldn't be able to stop the students from going to the trenches without turning the school into a jail, they sent the delinquent students to the basic military training camps; there the students would be under strict military discipline until they were eighteen, at which point they could choose whether to join the combatants in the front lines.

One critical factor that made the governance of this many students possible with relatively loose discipline was almost certainly the great trust that the students placed in Beraki. From other teachers, I learned that he had been a wonderful teacher, unusually kind and unbiased. When any students had some serious grievance, Beraki was always available to listen to their side of the story and, if necessary, adjudicate conflicts. He met with the students at least once a week to discuss issues affecting them, the teachers, and the school. All the students regarded him as a fair-minded friend and mentor who respected each of them as individuals. And he never abandoned his ideological commitments—which, I gathered, was a form of democratic socialism tempered by egalitarianism.

When Beraki left his position as head of the Education Department to become Minister of Information, his students gave him a goodbye party. On that occasion, a group of students carried him over their heads like they might have carried an ancient Grecian hero and paraded him through the crowd as a measure of their respect and affection.

The Literacy Campaign

Reflecting on Eritrea's history during precolonial, colonial, and now neocolonial domination, the EPLF identified an even greater threat to a democratic society than a foreign occupation army. Over 90 percent of the population was not just illiterate, but illiterate in nine different languages derived from at least six qualitatively different language families. Some of the languages had their own unique orthography (Ge'ez, Arabic, Roman alphabet); others had never been written. The EPLF considered the ability to read so important that it made literacy a requirement for anyone seeking to participate in the independence struggle. Volunteers who were illiterate when they first joined were required to attend literacy classes even in the trenches.

With the slogan "Illiteracy Is Our Arch Enemy" always in the back of their minds as a guiding principle, EPLF teachers organized literacy classes for the combatants in the early 1970s. By 1978, the Front had established 150 local schools throughout the liberated areas, where more than thirty thousand children of peasants and agro-pastoralists received an elementary school education. In predominantly Muslim regions, teachers tried to convince parents to let their daughters attend coeducational classes without having to wear the traditional Muslim veil. Although Muslim fathers objected strongly to this interference in their religious practices, these early efforts later became a catalyst for the emancipation of Eritrean women of all faiths.

For its part, the Education Department at the Zero School launched a universal literacy campaign whereby more than 450 of its advanced students crossed over into rural areas of the occupied zones to live with the peasants and teach them basic literacy skills. When the students demonstrated that it is possible for old farmers to learn from young students, the program was greatly enlarged, eventually reaching fifty-six thousand adults, 60 percent of whom were women. Zero School students were now teaching the peasants reading, writing, Eritrean history, hygiene, sanitation, and health maintenance. At the same time, they were expected to work directly with the peasants as a constant reminder that they were fortunate, and that their responsibility as such was not simply to work hard in their academic lessons but also to prepare themselves to contribute to the enormous task of lifting the Eritrean peasants out of abject poverty.

However, major changes in the military situation put those students participating in the cross-border educational program at increasingly unacceptable risks. For their safety, the program operating in the occupied or contested regions of Eritrea had to be abandoned. But that did not stop the continuing education of children and adults in the liberated areas.

The Reach of Education

To show me just how broadly the Education Department conceived of an Eritrean curriculum for Eritrean children, Joe brought me to a very large, well-camouflaged facility on the edge of the School campus that looked on the outside like an airplane hangar. Inside, however, the building was filled to the rafters with violins, violas, cellos, base fiddles, kettle drums, brass, and woodwinds—in other words, all the instruments that make up a well-equipped Western symphony orchestra. There was even a concert grand piano that had survived the trek from Port Sudan. Many of its strings were broken, reminding me of the telephone wires flapping in the wind on the road to Tokar.

Most of the instruments looked like they had never been played, and I wondered whether anyone at the Zero School even knew how to play them. As it turned out, there had once been a music teacher named YaAsina, who had graduated from the music school in Asmara. His plan was to train Eritrean students in Western-style music and establish a symphony orchestra that would modernize Eritrean music and perform it at a level that everyone would be able to understand. But this plan created a rift between him and the cadres, so he left the EPLF and ultimately made his way to the Zero School. Now, in a little shack that had been the administration building for the Music Department, an old fighter was coaching several students to play the instrument of their choice. From one direction came the shrill squeaks of a clarinet as one student diligently practiced his scales; from another direction came the grunts of a French horn grappling with difficult passages of classical music; and in yet another corner, someone was teaching a young girl how to hold her violin bow. The cacophony of sounds drifting over the silent desert was suggestive of a Dali painting.

I couldn't imagine what what would have motivated a lover of the arts, a rich donor, or a well-meaning patriot to spend a fortune to bring an entire symphony orchestra six to eight thousand miles across impossible terrain when there was no one at the destination who had any idea what to do with the instruments. Evidently, my exploration of the independence struggle had not reached deep enough to help me understand who might have embarked upon such a mission or how the importation of those instruments could further the cause of freedom and independence. But, undoubtedly, somebody, for some reason, had thought it could, and YaAsina and his students were very serious about their music lessons. Several years later, a few of the combatants vaguely remembered hearing something like a full orchestra playing a program of two or three classical pieces that actually sounded professional. But no one could recall who the conductor might have been or where he got a full professional orchestra.

Teaching Prisoners of War

On another day Joe took me to a very different corner of the school perimeter to show me how seriously the EPLF took literacy as a prime instrument for supporting political change. There, a small group of young men were reading, writing, cooking, playing volleyball, doing their laundry, or just relaxing. They looked a little different from most of the Eritreans I had met so far, but I couldn't pinpoint exactly why. Much more striking was the difference in their behavior, particularly the leisurely pace at which they carried on with whatever they were doing. I assumed that these must be EPLF combatants on a furlough of rest and relaxation, but Joe reminded me that there would be no R&R until the enemy had been defeated once and for all. Then he explained that these were former Ethiopian soldiers who had served their two-year terms as prisoners of war and were now free to go home. But almost to a man (there were no female soldiers in the Ethiopian armed forces), they refused to go home, as they knew they would be executed by their own officers as Eritrean spies or cowards. Again, most of them were illiterate Oromo boys who had been forced to join the front lines without training and usually without weapons. They had no stake in the territorial ambitions of their emperor, and, not surprisingly, they had either deserted or surrendered to the EPLF, often in division strength.

The thousands of Ethiopian ex-POWs who refused to be repatriated and had asked for political asylum presented the EPLF with a serious logistical problem. As long as they were legally POWs, they had to be guarded and fed according to the Geneva Convention. This imposed a severe burden on limited EPLF food supplies, given the major food shortages throughout the rural areas. But now these former combatants were no longer POWs. Nevertheless, they were allowed to stay in Eritrea and settle in small enclaves throughout the liberated areas, provided they worked for their keep like everyone else in the field. And since almost none of them had ever gone to school, they were also required to attend regular classes in reading and writing for four hours a day, five days a week. Teaching Ethiopian ex-POWs how to read and write went far beyond the requirements of the Geneva Convention.

But the EPLF took an interesting step further in treating these Ethiopian ex-soldiers with respect. The Education Department didn't just teach the POWs to read and write; it taught them in Amharic, the official language of Ethiopia. While it would have been far more convenient for the Tigrinya-speaking combatants to teach the Ethiopians in Tigrinya, they deliberately taught the Ethiopians to read and write in the language of their native country so that they would be prepared to join the Ethiopian opposition once it was safe for them to return home.

Mental Health at the Zero School

Ever since hordes of emotionally starved infants had overrun me during my first visit to the Solomuna orphanage, I had wondered how these children would adapt once they transferred to the Zero School and encountered its very different social demands and academic expectations. Having read a number of studies of what happens to children who spend their most vulnerable formative years in an institution, I expected that many of them would continue to carry heavy emotional scars long after their traumatic experiences in early childhood.

To my surprise, the opposite seemed to be the case. What impressed me most about the Zero School students and graduates was how open and direct, friendly yet dignified, they had become in their relationships with peers, teachers, and even strangers. To some observers, they were perhaps even *too* open and direct.

One afternoon, some of the older students, using internationally recognizable gestures, invited me to join them for lunch in their outdoor "cafeteria"—a long line of rocks well camouflaged under some trees and bushes. On another day, they invited me to join them in soccer practice, graciously ignoring the fact that I was hopelessly out of their league.

After spending an average of three or four years in the large Solomuna orphanage—which, by conventional criteria, would probably be rated as a bad place for raising children—the Zero School students had adapted remarkably well to very different and difficult social and physical circumstances. Watching them in their daily routine not only in the classroom but also in the bakery, in their construction work, in their agricultural pursuits, and on the soccer field (which had to be camouflaged with branches after every game), I saw that the bizarre "attachment" behavior that had been so overwhelming during my early visits to Solomuna had disappeared completely.

To get some idea about why the Zero School had been so successful preparing thousands of orphans for an unpredictable future, we asked some of the older combatants who had boarded their own children at the Zero School what they thought might explain the remarkably rapid, almost miraculous improvement in the orphans' psychological well-being.

Some parents attributed the dramatic recovery to the fact that the teachers treated all students, orphans or not, with respect, as if they were equal members of an extended family. This had given the children a sense of personal worth that they might otherwise never have experienced in a traditional family setting. Most of the students agreed that their teachers were always kind to them. But the teachers expected the same respect from the students and never coddled them. The parents were also convinced that, with the support of the teachers, the children who had been orphaned at an early age had largely overcome all their emotional and social difficulties, especially their inability to trust adults. Moreover, sharing confidences strengthened the children's self-confidence and helped them endure the hardships and uncertainties of their everyday lives. Some speculated that the orphans were actually better off than their own children because the orphans had made peace with the fact that their parents would never come back, while their own children had to separate from their parents at the end after every visit and then worry anew whether they would ever see them again.

Still other parents attributed the children's well-being to "natural" values of the EPLF, which the school was instilling in the children in ways that were age appropriate. Some were convinced that even the seven or eight-year-old students who had transferred from Solomuna were mature enough to understand that the EPLF was fighting not only for Eritrean independence but also for a better future for the next generation, and that it was this belief that kept them resilient. By contrast, Eritrean civilians who had been raised on traditional social values seemed to be offended by the students' directness, openness, and lack of guile, tending to deem such behavior as aberrant, symptomatic of a bad upbringing or an unhappy childhood. But the teachers had showed the students that they were part of a major social revolution for justice and independence.

When I asked Joe about his thoughts on this issue, he was fairly confident that the students had been through enough real experiences during their years at the school that it would have been very difficult to fill their heads with sloganeering rhetoric. He described how, in the early years, when the school had only a skeleton staff and most of the teachers had no formal teacher training, there was no Eritrean curriculum to replace the punitive Amharic curriculum that had been forced on the children. Instead, teachers and students had to rely on a traditional (and probably out-of-date) British curriculum. Moreover, the serious shortage of trained teachers and combatants who could function as counselors left the children feeling aimless and confused.

So it was hardly a surprise that during those early, turbulent years of adolescence, antisocial behavior took root. Small gangs of boys would ambush the trucks carrying freshly baked bread from the central bakery to the Zero School and either distribute it among gang members or sell it to other students for "favors." As the gangs got bolder, they adopted the harsher term *omerta*—meting out punishment when, for example, someone (girls as well as boys) who had joined a gang, then wanted to resign, and refused to obey the orders of the "head man" (or *capo*). In a notorious case known to the entire student body, a girl who refused to obey the orders of a bully classmate was severely beaten and lost one eye. Her mother, working in the nearby refugee camp, demanded to know what had happened to her, but the girl was so terrified by the threat of retaliation (the students used the word *overtax*) that she said nothing until a detailed investigation identified the bully, who was severely punished.

But as more and more Zero School teachers understood the underlying principles of learning by action, they created an egalitarian atmosphere that respected the individuality of each student and teacher. In this milieu, serious antisocial behavior steadily decreased and had, for all practical purposes, been eradicated. Around the same time, the frequency of air raids diminished considerably, not that there is any plausible linkage.

Joe had befriended many of the Zero School students and probably knew more about their emotional state than anyone else there. From his experience, he was convinced that, in any boarding school where hundreds of adolescent and teenage boys and girls were living together in a harsh and crowded environment, it was probably inevitable that some students would have serious psychosocial and emotional difficulties. Perhaps the surprise was not that some children indeed had such problems but, rather, that the total number of children with significant psychological problems was remarkably small for the size of the population.

As one might have expected, a few of the five thousand students had a hard time adapting to life at the Zero School. Most of those with apparent psychological problems seemed to have difficulty coping with the uncertainties of daily life and the future. Sometimes they exploded in a rage or burst into tears for no apparent reason. Since there were no trained psychologists and very few trained social workers at the school, the staff had to rely almost entirely on the spirit of cooperation among the students and between students and teachers, social workers, cooks, nurses, and the like, who formed a kind of "therapeutic community." Joe thought that most of the behavioral symptoms, anxieties, and oppositional behavior that he observed there would be expected in any boarding school; and most of the interpersonal conflicts and emotional symptoms were easily resolved by relying on the community's social supports and other forms of "milieu therapy" that did not require the services of a psychologist or psychiatrist.

One week at the Zero School was obviously much too short for me to form even a superficial impression of how Eritrea's children were being educated as the vanguard of the next generation. But that short time was enough to convince me that these students had adapted far better to the hardships of life at the Zero School than I would have predicted on the basis of what we think we understand about the long-terms effects of profound deprivation and the interminable exposure to violence.

Notes

1. Jean Piaget, in *To Understand Is to Invent: The Future of Education*, trans. George-Anne Roberts (New York: Grossman Press, 1972), 88.
2. Eleanor Duckworth, *The Having of Wonderful Ideas: And Other Essays on Teaching and Learning*, 3rd ed. (New York: Teachers College Press, 2006).
3. See Gottesman, *To Fight and to Learn*.

· 1 0 ·
CASSANDRA'S LIST

During the last few months of the war, everyone was focused on military victory and the blessings that peace would bring, and few Eritreans gave much thought to what would actually happen once the shooting stopped. Assefaw and I had often talked about Eritrea's future and whether the EPLF could assemble a democratic government that would steer the newly independent country through the dangerous passage from war to peace. Assefaw thought that some regression was probably inevitable, but that the people of Eritrea had suffered and sacrificed too much to let that regression get out of control. He urged us to do some "political soul searching" and explore the experience of other nations that had undergone the same experience. But I was convinced that, even if Eritrea was special, the fate of almost forty newly emerging African states that had made promising beginnings, only to descend into a morass of corruption and dictatorship, suggested that the transition from war to peace would be much more difficult than that from peace to war.[1]

Since Assefaw's prediction of relatively minor and reversible regressions didn't seem satisfactory, I spent some time in a large university library to research how other newly independent countries had fared. To my surprise, the library had very few books on the subject. I did, however, manage to compile a list of concrete issues that might impede a smooth transition from war to a sustainable peace so that Assefaw and I could continue to discuss the issues on my next visit.

By the time I returned to Eritrea in 1991, the EPLF had made substantial military progress, and the Ethiopian army, headed for a crushing defeat, had carpet-bombed Massawa in retaliation. Assefaw, who was now in charge of the health services in Massawa, had come to realize that far too little attention had been paid to what would happen once the enemy was overthrown. Hoping to provoke some active discussion on the point, he had distributed my paper to leading members of the EPLF—among them, the head of the military, the head of intelligence, the head of logistics, and all members of the politburo, as well as a knowledgeable Eritrean Relief Association representative—who had assembled in Massawa to plan the last and, with any luck, decisive battle against the remnants of the Ethiopian army. He had also arranged for me to participate in the discussion.

To ensure a relaxed context, he planned a festive dinner in a modern villa overlooking the Red Sea. (The villa had once belonged to the Italian beer baroness Madame Melloti.) The image of these leading veteran combatants who had known nothing but war for the last few decades sitting around an elegant table covered with fine Italian linen and silver flatware, eating special Eritrean delicacies, drinking Madame Melotti's last bottle of wine, and patiently listening to some foreign visitor's assessment of their country as they were planning a major assault on the remaining Ethiopian garrison troops was vintage Eritrean and vintage Assefaw.

On the basis of my limited library research and knowledge of Eritrea, I presented the following issues for their consideration.

The Diaspora

Thousands of families escaped the war by seeking shelter in the refugee camps of Sudan, where they have been living for many years. Despite effective cross-border operations conducted by the Eritrean Relief Committee, these families have been isolated for years from the social and political developments in Eritrean society. They have had to rely on the generosity of foreign governmental and nongovernmental relief agencies for food, water, and medical care and, as they have depended more and more on Arabic as their means of communication, their cultural ties to Eritrean society have weakened. When the time is right for their return to Eritrea, they will encounter a society that expects all its citizens to take personal responsibility for their own food and shelter as well as for the larger community. Unless measures are taken at the community level to help them overcome their cultural alienation and economic dependence, the returnees may be maligned as freeloaders and intruders.

The Postwar Society

The war has united combatants and civilians, men and women, farmers and nomads, students and teachers, Coptic Christians and Muslims, and (within limits) seven ethnic groups with different languages and cultural traditions in their struggle against an external enemy. This struggle has forged a spirit of cooperation and solidarity across the different groups, giving them an unprecedented sense of Eritrean nationhood. But what will sustain this spirit of cooperation and solidarity once the external enemy is defeated? Will the old power struggles between the EPLF and ELF, between Christians and Muslims, be revived to frustrate the national goal of a unified sovereign state? Will the external enemy who once united all Eritreans be replaced by a pernicious internal enemy that rules from the top down and divides the country against itself? What can be done even before the war is over to prevent the disintegration of a united Eritrean front?

Demobilization

Every country that has ever fought a prolonged war must in one way or another take into consideration the thousands of young adults who survived the killing and now expect to be compensated for their years of service and sacrifice. Many governments have acknowledged their obligation to veterans in principle, but few have made wise choices in this regard. Pensions or cash bonuses run the danger of turning unemployed veterans into psychological cripples. How will the new government support those who have dedicated the most productive years of their lives to the independence war?

Many of the EPLF combatants, including those who never went to school before joining the Front, have acquired great technical skills in a variety of pursuits during their years in the base camps, and their skills will be crucial to Eritrea's social and economic reconstruction after the war. For example, the child-care counselors who transformed the Solomuna orphanage into a child-centered residential setting will be urgently needed to care for many thousands of orphans after independence. Similarly, the barefoot doctors who were largely responsible for the success of the grassroots health services could play a vital role in establishing a nationwide program of primary health services. However, these counselors and doctors have no official papers (certificates, diplomas) to document the knowledge and experience they gained in the field, and the value of the skills they acquired might well be discounted in a peacetime society. Replacing them with "real" counselors and doctors who, although formally trained in child psychology and curative medicine, have no understanding of the needs of traumatized children and war-weary civilians would be a strategic error.

Combatants, Women, and the Civil Society

For almost three decades, the Ethiopian military controlled a large sector of the Eritrean population in the urban centers and other occupied zones through fear, suspicion, and corruption. Using various propaganda techniques, it made a concerted effort to corrupt Eritrea's young people in those areas with sex, alcohol, pornography, and the like, and it deliberately kept captive Eritreans ignorant of what was happening in the world. By contrast, the combatants and civilians in the liberated areas of Eritrea have undergone a radical transformation, attaining a kind of political "maturity." In effect, two subcultures have emerged with disparate values and social expectations.

Social norms of conduct that were not only acceptable in wartime but even adaptive and essential for survival in the field will likely clash with the more traditional norms of behavior and morality adhered to by civilians. What steps can be taken now and in the future to minimize the impact of an inevitable "culture clash" between those who have survived in the urban centers by submitting to authority, at least superficially, and those who "never knelt down" but remained fiercely independent and built an EPLF subculture?

This culture clash will likely be most dramatic among the young women who joined the Front and then returned to their families. Nearly all liberationist struggles in the twentieth century have been committed to the proposition that progressive revolutions will succeed only when women are guaranteed the same social, political, and economic rights by law as men. Yet few, if any, revolutions have put this proposition into practice once the shooting has ended and women are no longer needed as combatants.

What might the Eritrean women expect in their struggle for equality after the war? What measures can both men and women take at this critical time to ensure that the political and economic gains women have made during the war can be sustained? Enforcing gender equality by proclamation or law will almost certainly not work; on the contrary, it will alienate large segments of the population, male as well as female. But if women are unable to achieve the equality for which they have long fought, what will that mean for the survival of the new, independent nation-state?

The potential culture clash is especially critical where the children are concerned. Those who grew up in the base camps, and particularly those who were raised by the community, assimilated the values and modes of conduct of the combatants, their role models. Finding it difficult to adapt to traditional social norms, they might end up engaging in behavior that is deemed antisocial.

Unaccompanied Children

If the experience in many other countries throughout the world, and especially after World War II, is any indication, the cities and towns of postwar Eritrea will be flooded with orphans, abandoned children, street children, gangs of delinquents, and "sex workers" who gravitate naturally to urban centers because they have no place else to go and are probably illiterate. The number of children and adolescents in especially difficult circumstances after thirty years of war will exceed by several orders of magnitude the number of orphans and other rootless children successfully nurtured by the ASA in the base camps. To combat this problem, the ASA has instituted a program to reunify orphans with their extended families or, should no extended families be located, with neighbors or close family friends. However, the war has left many Eritrean families so poor that they are not able to feed their own children, much less take in orphaned relatives. Will a scaled-up version of this program be sufficient to address the upbringing and social needs of these orphaned children, or will new problems emerge, such as antisocial behavior and gang formation, that will require entirely different solutions?

The Leadership

The history and eventual fate of almost all twentieth-century revolutions should leave even the most dedicated leftist with a strong suspicion that the leaders of armed independence struggles—those who have either been chosen by due process or risen to leadership by other means—inevitably prove reluctant to relinquish their positions of power after the first phase of the revolutionary process has ended and the guns are silent. Rather, they seem compelled by some evolutionary quirk or developmental mistake of human beings to take all necessary steps to consolidate and expand their power base, eliminate those who might threaten their authority, and abandon the once-promised principles of collective leadership and replace them with a centralized autocracy that rules from the top down.

Authoritarian patterns of governance may be adaptive in wartime—a central source of power must be willing to give commands, painful and terrifying as such authority might be. But when the same authoritarian structure persists in peacetime and becomes institutionalized as the norm, it becomes counterproductive and insidiously plants the seeds of its own destruction. Generals who are reluctant to give up their authority may elevate themselves to the position of marshal and, if they deem it necessary, trigger an armed coup d'état that will give them dictatorial powers. Once they have consolidated their power, they will have no difficulty claiming, or in some cases actually precipitating, continuing emergencies and social unrest to justify their one-man rule. This seems to have been the outcome of the Bolshevik revolution under Lenin and then Stalin, of leftist revolutions in many Eastern Europe and some Asian countries, and of nearly all newly emerging countries in Sub-Saharan Africa. The fate of Eritrea's children, who will inherit the fruits of the independence struggle, will ultimately depend on the current leadership's ability to exercise restraint and cede power in a timely fashion to the next generation when its reign is no longer productive.

The combatants sitting around Madame Melotti's table had spent decades discussing the political structure of *their* revolution, how it differed from most other African independence movements, and what the pros and cons of either a socialist or a capitalist form of government were. Now they graciously listened to my presentation, discussed each of my concerns seriously, and commented thoughtfully. The commander-in-chief of all military campaigns, for example, insisted that military rank meant nothing to him except when it was a matter of discipline, and he doubted very much that rank meant anything more to any of the EPLF cadres. He further insisted that he would leave military service behind as soon as possible after the war ended; that he had no interest in a military career or, for that matter, in a political career based on his military service. And he doubted very much whether any of the other fighters would try to stay in the army after a stable peace had been achieved. All the military cadres had grown up in rural areas, as the children of peasants or workers. None of the commanders had been trained in or graduated from war colleges, as had nearly all English-speaking and French generals. There was no such thing as an hereditary military caste such as, for example, in Germany before and during World War II. The chief of all intelligence and internal security similarly insisted that those who—purely from necessity—were currently in leadership positions had no political ambitions or desire to consolidate their power; they just wanted to get on with their lives.

The women's point of view was not fairly represented at the table, the only women present being those who had cooked and served the meal and yet were not eating with us. Several of the men challenged my comments on women's future after the war. One noted that "handing over" power to women would never work and that unless women fought for their rights, any improvement in their status would be merely temporary. No doubt he was right, but when I suggested that there was nothing to prevent men from supporting rather than opposing women in their struggle for equality, he countered that, in that case, women "would want too much."

As might have been expected, their main criticism of my presentation was that I relied far too much on the emotional aspects of war and on the psychological dimensions of individual combatants—the human factor—rather than on the objective, historical realities of a postcolonial class structure in the larger context of international politics and the Cold War. They were actually right, although perhaps not quite in the way they meant.

For my list of issues I had chosen—without having any particular target in mind—whatever came to mind about the transition from war to peace that was or seemed most immediately relevant to the Eritrean case. However, I ended up emphasizing problems and issues that are of universal human concern and would have major political implications for the future of Eritrea's children. Only time would tell whether the cautions raised and the possible consequences implied would be taken seriously by the new government once the last battle in Massawa had been won and everyone realized that they were now free to go home.

Note

1 Martin Meredith, *The Fate of Africa: A History of Fifty Years of Independence* (New York: Public Affairs, 2005).

· 1 1 ·

PEACE AT LAST

The end of the thirty-year war was marked by the bloody battle for Massawa. Eritrea was now an independent country *de facto*, if not yet *de jure*. By 1991 the outcome of the referendum—whether the people of Eritrea wanted total independence or federation with Ethiopia—was a foregone conclusion: about 99.8 percent of the population wanted complete independence. UN observers at the polling stations all confirmed that the voting had been fair. However, Eritrea's independence was not officially declared until 1993.

Since there was as yet no elected transitional government, the EPLF cadres filled the key positions by choosing, from their own roster of commanders, individuals to fill the key positions that would in time constitute Eritrea's first provisional government. Isaias Afwerki, who had been chosen Secretary General of the EPLF Central Committee during the liberation struggle, still enjoyed enormous popularity and was later unanimously elected president. Some referred to Isaias[1] as the George Washington of Eritrea.

When the EPLF marched into Asmara in 1991, the country's infrastructure was in ruins. The treasury was empty. Electricity and running water were available for only a few hours every day. The toilets didn't flush. The sewers, which had been built with great skill by the Italian engineers, were filled to overflowing with garbage and untreated sewage. Most of the wards of the

Central Hospital in the center of Asmara had been left intact by the departing Ethiopian soldiers, but they were so filthy that it might take years before they could receive patients.

Even apart from that, the fledgling government faced enormous challenges. The broad outlines of a postwar agenda of political, social, and economic policies, formulated in 1987 at the Second Eritrean Congress, called for pluralism, participatory democracy, a multiparty system, and an economy based on liberal trade formulas. But now the dream of a liberated Eritrea had to be turned into a concrete reality, and the gaps between dream and reality were enormous. Having barely recovered from the long, devastating war, the provisional government had to make hard decisions about defense against not only an external enemy but also against the germinating internal enemies of corruption and superstition. Many thousands of combatants expected to be demobilized within the foreseeable future, but the new government lacked the financial resources to compensate them for their many years of loyal service or offer them any promise of employment except to keep them in the civil service.

But here and there were optimistic signs that Eritrea might be on the road to recovery. The damaged harbor facilities in Massawa and Assab had been temporarily repaired, so that ships from abroad could bring in the urgently needed supplies for reconstruction. Plans to enlarge these facilities were already on the drawing board. The country's major roads, also built long ago by Italian structural engineers, had remained largely intact until the heavy Ethiopian tanks chewed up the asphalt surface. However, very soon after independence, road crews were busy repairing, widening, and resurfacing the main roads connecting Asmara and Massawa.

In Asmara, most of the city's public buildings, including the celebrated Art Deco buildings in the city center, had been spared the effects of the war. The upscale villas in the best residential quarters, where Ethiopian officers had once been billeted, were now being repaired, prettified, and appropriated by the ranking EPLF cadres—the first hint of the creeping corruption in the EPLF leadership—although the rank-and-file fighters had no place to live. There were enough basic food staples in the open-air markets to ensure that no one was starving, and there were no beggars on the streets apart from the street urchins. The many pharmacies on the main streets were overflowing with all the latest remedies for all sorts of real and imaginary ailments. A battalion of old women swept the streets every morning, leading foreign visitors to compare the streets favorably with those of other African capital cities.

The sidewalk cafes, dating back to the Italian colonial period, had been repaired and repainted and were already serving excellent espresso and sweet buns. Every afternoon, older Eritrean gentlemen dressed in shiny, outdated, but still elegant suits and fedoras filled the espresso bars and pastry shops as they discussed the good and not-so-good old days of the Italian era and the latest political scandals. New bars quickly popped up everywhere and were filled to capacity within two or three days after opening. A few souvenir shops were open for business, selling postcards of the famous railroad from Massawa to Asmara, although there were no tourists to buy them yet.

But tourists quickly took advantage of favorable currency exchange rates and began to return to Asmara and Massawa in increasing numbers. A fledgling Ministry of Tourism organized tours to the Dalak Islands in the Red Sea, where visitors could snorkel for exotic tropical fish. The Red Sea Corporation, the commercial branch of the political party, built several modern hotels on the beaches of Massawa. Swimming and sunbathing again became favorite diversions for both rich Eritreans and foreign visitors, while older Italians who had once lived in Eritrea returned and bought up the beachfront properties that Eritreans could no longer afford. Restaurants serving traditional Eritrean or Italian or Chinese food were popping up everywhere at the rate of almost one a week, as were pizza parlors. Well-to-do Eritrean visitors from abroad and foreigners made the rounds from one restaurant to the next, looking for the newest and therefore the best.

Blue-collar crime was unheard of. It was taken as a matter of fact that Eritreans simply didn't steal, wouldn't lie, and didn't dream of armed robbery. Unarmed policemen strolled leisurely up and down the main boulevards, spending their time looking for traffic violators and disentangling the constant traffic jams caused by the sudden influx of second-hand cars. These traffic jams and the foul black smoke belching from the ancient Italian buses that ferried people from one end of Asmara to the other for a few pennies were the irrefutable signs that Eritrea was on the road to recovery. The only weapons to be seen on the streets were Kalashnikovs toted by two soldiers guarding the entrance to the reopened Commercial Bank of Eritrea, and I suspect that their rifles were not even loaded. Foreign visitors, especially young women associated with European NGOs, all remarked on how safe they felt when walking alone at night.

By 1993, the government was publishing one official newspaper in Tigrinya and English, followed by independently published newspapers in Tigrinya, Arabic, and English. Peace Corps volunteers, who had always been welcome in Eritrea during the federation era of the 1950s, were welcomed again and resumed teaching English as a second language. Everyone wanted to study English, to secure a good job or have an opportunity for advancement.

International relief organizations, national and international development agencies, and NGOs were flocking to Asmara in droves—settling themselves in the best villas, hiring their own nationals at extravagant salaries, promoting all kinds of social, agricultural, and medical projects, and writing long reports to the home office to keep the money coming. The new Eritrean government, however, fed up with this state of affairs, threw out all the NGOs—including, unfortunately, those experienced, seriously committed organizations that respected local customs and traditional culture and sought to be useful by collaborating with their Eritrean colleagues.

By 1992, when I returned to Eritrea to continue my study of the orphans, it was possible to fly directly from Frankfurt to Asmara, thereby bypassing the endless border crossings from Sudan. As we circled over the airport, preparing to land, I finally saw the famous capital city of Asmara—Eritrea's Jerusalem—for the first time. The plane was packed with Eritreans from Europe, North America, and the Middle East who had been separated from their families for several decades and finally had the opportunity to return home for a visit. The moment the plane landed, its door opened and the passengers swept down the gangway. Old women who could barely walk rushed out of the plane, pushed other passengers aside, knelt on the ground, said a prayer, and kissed the earth of Eritrea before limping off as fast as they could to embrace the families they had left behind.

Nerayo and Assefaw had come to the airport to welcome me and ensure that the computers I had brought with me didn't get lost. Enormous crowds were dancing in hysterical jubilation, drinking away the night in the overflowing bars. But Nerayo and Assefaw had no stomach for celebration; too many of their friends had been killed in the war. They didn't say so, but I suspect that they were also worried that Ethiopia would never give up its claim to free access to the Red Sea and would try again to secure it.

To savor peace after decades of war, citizens of Asmara liked to drive up to the highest point of the escarpment above the city and drink locally distilled Araki at a popular bar. Assefaw had found a rocky little path away from the crowd, where only an occasional peasant bringing his goats home interrupted the solitude. There we would sit quietly in the evening, watching the pure white cloudbanks drifting in from the east as the sun set behind the mountains. Sometimes we could see regions on the horizon where it was raining.

The entire hillside around us was full of one- and two-story-high cactus plants that in some seasons were full of prickly pears, which the street children would harvest and then sell for a few pennies.

Sometimes Assefaw would tell me about the campaigns they had fought on the edges of these steep canyons, which made everyone dizzy if they looked down. Somewhere hidden in these deep valleys had been the terrain where Yemane Dawit had set up his first aid stations and then a regional hospital, as well as the place where Assefaw and his colleagues had first practiced trauma surgery while evading roving Ethiopian patrols. Sometimes we talked about the size of the universe, what lay on the other side of the Milky Way, the grassroots health-care system in North Vietnam, the pros and cons of the death penalty, and whether and how hypnosis works. It didn't really matter what we talked about in this awesome silence; the stark beauty of the unforgiving mountains and valleys was enough to fuel conversation now that Eritrea was at peace.

One evening, Assefaw decided that these peaceful surroundings were an ideal place for enjoying coffee in the Eritrean tradition. There were no coffeehouses in our isolated place on the top of the escarpment, but he knew where to go. He walked across the goat path to a shack built out of rocks taken from the mountainside, pieces of corrugated iron, and straw mats that kept out most of the rain, and he politely knocked on the wooden frame. A dog of mixed heritage barked furiously at us until a rail-thin young woman in rags came out to see what the commotion was about.

Eden was still a young woman, but the years of hard labor and of feeding and clothing her family had taken their toll. Yet when Assefaw asked her if she might prepare the coffee ceremony for us, her face lit up in a beautiful smile and she was a young girl again. She happily went through the whole elaborate ceremony without leaving out a single detail. When the coffee was ready, she poured each of us the traditional three small cups sweetened with mountains of sugar, and she burned a few precious crystals of incense that enveloped us in a churchlike aroma.

After that, we would regularly drive up to the escarpment to drink Eden's ceremonial coffee. On special days, she would add a bowl full of freshly popped popcorn, which was now an integral feature of the ceremony. One evening, when it was too cold to sit outside, Eden invited us to drink inside her shack, where six or seven people were already sleeping on the floor in front of the fire—an elderly couple, probably Eden's parents; a grown man who may have been Eden's husband; and three or four of her children. The dog, however, was not allowed inside.

It was a hard existence. Eden, who by all indicators was the one who kept the family together, accepted her lot as her destiny. The neighborhood shunned her and her family because one of her children had an Ethiopian father. But Assefaw respected her for her iron will and admired her peasant strength.

Note

1 As a note appended to Martin Plaut's *Newsweek* article "Who Is Isaias Afwerki, Eritrea's Enigmatic Dictator?" explains, "Eritreans are known by their first names, so Isaias Afwerki is known as President Isaias on second reference." See *Newsweek*, November 1, 2016, http://www.newsweek.com/who-isaias-afwerki-eritreas-enigmat-ic-dictator-515761

Part II
ONE HUNDRED THOUSAND ORPHANS

· 1 2 ·

MEETING THE CHALLENGE

Before the war, Eritrean families had always taken it for granted that they would be responsible for nurturing, feeding, and protecting any children who had lost their parents as long as those children were members of the extended family. However, after three decades of war, the number of orphans in urgent need of protection, care, and rehabilitation had increased exponentially and, now, far exceeded the number of families who could afford to feed and care for additional children when they could barely feed and care for their own. The ASA, later renamed the Ministry of Labour and Human Welfare (MLHW), had to address the problem of Eritrea's orphans and figure out how to reintegrate them into their communities.

To get some perspective on the scale of the problems that needed a remedy and the range of remedies that could be implemented relatively quickly, Assefaw, Yemane, and Gere took up the challenge of finding humane, sustainable, and affordable solutions to the orphan problem. After conducting a nationwide survey of all the urban centers and outlying regions of Eritrea that could be reached by Land Cruiser, they found that there were at least a hundred thousand orphans, street children (those who might or might not have families, but were on the streets trying to survive), children whose families had sent them into the streets to panhandle to support them, disabled children, and juvenile prostitutes. Of the hundred thousand children from two to sixteen years of age who were registered as being in need of special protections (one of every thirty Eritreans), ten thousand were war orphans; six thousand had lost both parents, had no living relatives, and were classified as "full" orphans; and about four thousand still had a living relative, but in many cases that relative was no longer physically or mentally able to care for young children. It seemed a foregone conclusion that those numbers would swell once the more than one-hundred-fifty thousand Eritrean refugee families returned from Sudan.

By relying on their own experience in the field and the number of children who were in urgent need of relief, Assefaw, Yemane, and Gere formulated a comprehensive plan for their care. Their plan—which integrated traditional cultural values, local child-rearing practices and patterns of family life, and current historical realities after the war, as well as the lessons learned in the Solomuna orphanage and at the Zero School—had three major components:

Orphanages

The MLHW had originally planned to permanently close all the orphanages, including Solomuna, as soon as possible after independence, but the number of children who urgently needed special protection far exceeded the number who could immediately be reunified with extended families. The MLHW had no choice but to renovate either one large or several smaller orphanages until the reunification program was fully under way.

When the EPLF marched into and liberated Asmara, about two thousand children were still living in sixteen institutions that had been supported by either the Ethiopian government or religious organizations that had worked in Eritrea for many years. These institutions varied in size from small facilities with fewer than thirty beds (with only one child to each), to the one state-run orphanage in Asmara that remained home for more than three hundred children up to age eighteen, to a mid-size orphanage in the countryside that could house up to two hundred residents and had integrated a working farm and a residential school for older children. These institutions differed widely in their styles of child management and parenting,[1] access to schools and social facilities for children, and so forth. An additional three thousand older children and young adolescents without parents had been placed in various academic and vocational boarding schools shortly after the war, but, since they were relatively well looked after, no definitive decision was made at the time about their long-term fate.

Reunification

The keystone of the Eritrean child-protection program would eventually become a community-based program for reunifying orphans with their extended families. This is essentially adoption with the important caveat that adoption was within families who were related by blood. In cases where there were no extended families to accept the orphan, neighbors or close family friends often accepted the responsibility. The reunification program was therefore based on traditional patterns of informal adoption that had been part of the rural culture for decades, perhaps even centuries.[2] However, a number of major hurdles had to be overcome before the reunification of orphans with host families could become a viable alternative.

Small Group Homes

The MLHW anticipated that there would almost certainly be orphans who, for various reasons, had no extended families—or at least none that were socially or physically able to care for them. As a safety net for these orphans, who were probably the most profoundly deprived of them all, the MLHW proposed to build a network of small group homes throughout the country where up to twelve children would live with one or two permanent housemothers.

With financial support from NGOs and international development agencies, these three major components of child protection were greatly expanded but without any loss of local community control over the everyday activities.

Notes

1 U. Ericsson, *A Profile of Orphanages in Eritrea* (Asmara, Eritrea: Authority of Social Affairs, Republic of Eritrea, 1985).
2 E. Morah, S. Mebrathu, and K. Sebhatu, "Evaluation of the Orphan Reunification Project in Eritrea," *Evaluation and Program Planning* 21, no. 4 (1998): 437–448.

· 1 3 ·

ORPHANAGES

In Western industrial or postindustrial societies, orphanages are generally viewed as relics that have been almost totally eliminated and replaced by formal adoption processes or, if necessary, foster care programs (although that also raises questions about the children's safety and protection). Yet, in the underdeveloped world as well as in Russia, Eastern Europe, the Middle East, China, and Latin America, fully functioning orphanages of various sizes abound.

What happens to young children who are cared for in large institutions? Child-development experts in Western societies have, over the centuries, reached a consensus that orphans, and especially young orphans, should never be placed in orphanages if there are any viable alternatives.[1] That conclusion has been reinforced in recent decades by many outcome studies of newborns and infants—for example, those who were warehoused in the notorious Romanian orphanages, where they "were deprived of virtually all human contact" and received only "minimal food, clothing, heat, or care givers."[2] That a large majority of orphanages put young children at greatly increased risk for psychopathology therefore hardly requires further confirmation.

Yet, while there is a plethora of reports to support the truism that bad orphanages are bad for children, far less attention has been paid to anecdotal and clinical evidence demonstrating that it is possible to create decent, affordable, and sustainable social environments for orphans even when resources are very limited. After reviewing all English-language reports on the effects of residential group care for unaccompanied children in North American institutions between 1930 and 1990, John McCall, for example, shows that much of the putative evidence that orphanages are invariably bad for children is far less convincing than the widespread consensus seems to imply.[3]

Richard McKenzie, who had himself grown up in an orphanage, arrived at a similar conclusion after interviewing twelve hundred middle-aged adults who had been raised in nine different North American orphanages.[4] Most had left the orphanages after graduating from high school, at which point their psychological, cognitive, and emotional development was, on average, at least as favorable as that of persons who had been raised by their own families in similar socioeconomic circumstances. When leaving the orphanages at age eighteen, the students unanimously agreed that they had never wanted to be adopted; and yet, only a small minority rated their orphanage less than favorably.

My point here is not to support the banal generalization that all orphanages are bad for children, or to proffer the parallel and equally banal generalization that good orphanages are good for children. My point is rather to suggest, on the basis of limited experience, that when there are no viable or humane alternatives, it is possible to establish decent child-centered orphanages for unaccompanied children who have nowhere else to go. That then leaves the question of vital interest throughout much of the developing world: when residential care offers such children the only hope of survival, what can be done to prevent the irreversible consequences of early deprivation?

To address this question, it is essential that child-care specialists determine what distinguishes good orphanages from bad ones. A comparison of different kinds of orphanages in different social environments may offer some clues. Since postwar Eritrea seemed like a favorable setting for arriving at some answers, Gere and I visited a relatively large number of orphanages that had developed qualitatively different styles of governance and philosophies of child protection.

The Asmara Children's Home

The largest of the remaining government-sponsored orphanages that had to be renovated after the war was the Asmara Children's Home. A complex facility built by the Italian colonial government, it had functioned until now as the Asmara Orphanage, a facility for Ethiopian children. From everything the combatants and child-care workers told me, it had provided a safe haven for orphans, operating under the control of different national governments, each with its own philosophy of child rearing. This orphanage probably came closest to representing the "traditional orphanage" of many benign clinical studies that did not provoke international outrage.

Located on the edge of the city, next to the airport, the Asmara Children's Home (having changed its name after the war because the label "orphanage" had a bad connotation) was able to accommodate about three hundred children up to eighteen years of age. A few adolescents and young adults who had grown up there were allowed to stay longer to finish their studies, so they could qualify for admission to the University of Asmara. Children above the age of seven were enrolled in one of the nearby public schools, where they mingled freely with children from the urban neighborhood. They were allowed to invite town children to play basketball and soccer in the large playground of the orphanage and were invited to visit town children in their homes during festival days and school vacations. Parents in the neighborhood brought sweets for the orphans on special days.

The main building of the orphanage was an imposing two-story stone structure with a large entrance and with offices and an auditorium on the first floor. On the second floor were about fifteen colorless dormitory rooms, each virtually barren except for beds and spring mattresses for fifteen to twenty same-age children. Older boys and girls slept in separate dormitories without supervision. Counselors who didn't sleep in the orphanage went home at night. As far as I could determine, the children had no place to keep their clothes, books, and other personal belongings—in fact, they didn't seem to *have* any personal belongings. Every morning, they picked out the clothes that they would wear that day from a large pile of washed clothes deposited on the floor of the dormitory.

Adjacent to the kitchen was a large dining hall where about sixty to seventy children ate in shifts. The counselors never sat down to eat with the children. In fact, there was an implicit yet distinct social boundary, with children on one side and teachers and administration on the other. The counselors who supervised the meals made sure that the children got enough to eat and helped those who were still too young to eat by themselves. When I visited, the cook, an enormous, gray-haired woman, was stirring whatever was bubbling in the open kettle. With a toothless grin, she offered me a sample of her porridge, but it didn't smell very good, so I declined and was grateful that she didn't insist.

Next to the kitchen was a large nursery, where an old nurse of some religious order was caring for ten to fifteen newborns who had been abandoned or left on somebody's doorstep. Together with her small staff of assistants, the Sister, who had worked at the orphanage throughout the Ethiopian occupation, and her small staff of assistants did their best to hold and comfort those infants. But, as in the Solomuna orphanage, there was always too much to do to keep the infants clean and fed and still provide them with the affection they so desperately craved. After only a week or two in the nursery, the infants exhibited the all-too-familiar signs of "hospitalism." Some rolled their heads monotonously back and forth until their scalps began to bleed and their heads had to be restrained; some still made a pathetic effort to reach out and make contact with another human being, while others turned their heads away from anyone who tried to comfort them or were too weak to even raise their arms to beg to be picked up. And a few had given up altogether and just stared at the ceiling.

Foundlings

Even before the war for independence, in Eritrea, as in almost all countries, there had always been abandoned newborns, but their numbers were always small and local social workers had always been able to find them a decent sanctuary where they could spend the critical years of their schooling in the public school systems. When war came, however, the number of these foundlings exploded.

In most cases, no one knew anything about the origin of these infants—their patronymic, village of birth, or social status of their putative families. In many cases, they were abandoned by young girls who had become pregnant and could not bear the shame of not being married. For a time, social workers from all corners of Eritrea began to bring these infants to the Asmara Orphanage on the pretext that their local facilities were inadequate to cope with the problem. As a result, by 1996, just a few years after independence had been achieved, the newborn nursery wing of the orphanage was horribly overcrowded and understaffed, conditions that were exacerbated by the prevalence of fevers of unknown origin, upper respiratory infections, and other diseases for which these infants required extra attention and, on occasion, isolation. To remedy the situation, a large hall in the auxiliary building had to be renovated to accommodate additional infants.

Knowing full well that these infants wouldn't live much longer unless drastic measure were taken to improve their care, the MLHW looked everywhere for viable alternatives. Public information messages were sent by national radio and television, informing middle-class families in Asmara and Massawa about opportunities for adopting young infants with a minimum of red tape, but these messages didn't make a dent in the cultural prejudices against adoption or foster care. From 1999 to 2004, only twenty-four orphans were adopted, and a much larger crop of newly abandoned infants quickly filled the cribs they had vacated.

A brand-new and very attractive nursery was built with generous funds from a Scandinavian NGO. This nursery consisted of eight large rooms, each equipped with an attached sunporch and room for six cribs. A staff of high school graduates was recruited to care for the orphans under the supervision of an experienced nurse; although these new counselors had received only very brief training, many had taken care of their younger siblings at home and so had some experience as child-care counselors. Nearby, the Ministry of Education built a wonderful new kindergarten, containing six airy rooms for eight to ten children each. It came with a university-trained teacher and a collection of attractive wooden toys that had been made in a large toyshop on the campus of the Asmara Orphanage; this toyshop eventually became a commercial enterprise, whose profits the MLHW used to support other improvements in the Asmara Children's Home. But it didn't take long before this new kindergarten was also hopelessly overcrowded.

Now desperately seeking a permanent solution, the MHLW began renovations on a set of buildings in the countryside. Mai Habar—once a leper colony, then a barracks for Ethiopian soldiers, and, after the war, a residence for severely disabled combatants—had several potential advantages. After renovation, it was projected to accommodate between four hundred and five hundred foundlings from birth to age five. The buildings were all only one story high, so the toddlers would never have to climb stairs. Moreover, the children would be living in the fresh air, near a large papaya orchard rather than in the growing smog of Asmara. A new school for social workers was already under construction that would, if all went according to plan, become the resource for many additional child-care workers.

Initially, the plan for Mai Habar seemed like a good short-term solution to the pressing problem of overcrowding. But unless additional measures were taken to stem the flood of abandoned babies, it too would soon be filled beyond capacity, duplicating the awful conditions that had prevailed for years in the Asmara Children's Home. And in these turbulent times of civil unrest, what was to be done with the hundreds of foundlings that no families were willing or able to adopt and give a chance at life?

About half of the staff in the Asmara Children's Home were civilians who had worked there during the war; the other half had been childcare counselors in Solomuna who had accompanied the orphans on their exodus from the base camps. Similarly, about half of the older children had lived in the orphanage during the Ethiopian occupation while the other half had been transferred from Solomuna.

The orphanage director had been appointed to this position immediately after the war. He had no experience working with children, was clearly out of his depth when it came to running an orphanage, and relied almost entirely on how the facility had been run by the Ethiopians. On the assumption that children who had lost their parents at an early age needed a well-structured environment, he had created a residential setting with explicit rules of conduct and a predictable daily schedule so that the children would always feel secure. By his own words, he favored an authoritarian leadership style, did not delegate responsibility, did not hold regular staff meetings, and made all decisions affecting the orphanage himself.

To get some idea of what effect this style of child rearing—probably the preferred model in orphanages for centuries—was having on the development and personalities of these children, Gere interviewed the counselors who had looked after the children in the original Asmara Orphanage and compared their perspectives on child-rearing practices with those of the counselors who had cared for and accompanied the children from Solomuna. He kept his interviews strictly confidential so that the counselors would feel free to speak openly.

As Gere learned, the counselors who had worked in the Asmara Orphanage during the war (hereinafter, for simplicity, referred to as the Asmara counselors) agreed with the headmaster that firm discipline and explicit rules of conduct were best for the orphans because it made them feel secure. But those who had accompanied the children from Solomuna (hereinafter, the Solomuna counselors) took strong exception to the headmaster's style of governance. They criticized him for having no feeling for children in especially difficult circumstances and no respect for their individuality, and for denying them the opportunity to make their own choices so that they could develop a sense of self-confidence and learn from their mistakes. They also objected to the demeaning ways in which the Asmara counselors disciplined the children with insulting remarks and unwarranted slapping, made the children follow instructions rather than reasoning with them, and didn't listen to them or help them solve their social and academic problems.

The Solomuna counselors described the orphans whom they had accompanied as self-confident, independent minded, outspoken (perhaps to the point of rudeness), and "democratic" in their social relationships. By contrast, they perceived the Asmara orphans as passive, submissive, overly dependent, and lacking in initiative and any self-esteem. The Asmara counselors, on their part, portrayed the Solomuna orphans as rude, disrespectful, brash, willful, headstrong, and in need of discipline, whereas they considered the orphans who had grown up in Asmara during the war as polite, obedient, and observant of social traditions with respect to adults.

Only time would tell whether the conflicting social values internalized by children even within one large institution were transient or permanent.

The Comboni School

The MLHW had transferred a group of about one hundred to one hundred fifty Solomuna orphans to the Comboni School in Asmara. Built by an Italian religious order as a day school for the children of the Italian families once living in Asmara, the Comboni School was later turned into an elementary school for those children. Once the foreign troops had been evacuated, the school was converted into a temporary boarding school for the Solomuna orphans as well as a day school for the children of EPLF cadres stationed in Asmara. So that the orphans being transferred would have a sense of continuity amid these bewildering changes, their counselors and teachers from the base camps accompanied them to the Comboni School and stayed with them there until more permanent placements could be found.

To see how well the orphans had weathered their transfer to the urban excitement of the center of Asmara, I visited the Comboni School on a sunny Sunday morning while the children were playing in the large school playground. Their counselors and teachers who had known them in Solomuna quickly saw that they had handled the long trip very well, had readily adapted to the strange environment of a big city, and were already outperforming most of the local home-reared children of EPLF cadres who now sat in the same classrooms with them.

I found a shady spot on the edge of the playground where I would not disturb the children while watching them play soccer or build castles from sand, mud, and water. But despite my efforts to remain unobtrusive, the children spotted me immediately. This time, however, they didn't rush over to compete for total physical contact or interrogate me as they might have done a year earlier. Rather, after giving me a passing glance, they returned to their games. Their ability to ignore a stranger—and a white stranger at that—seemed like a major advance in the maturation of their social relationships.

Ultimately, however, they couldn't contain themselves. First a courageous girl and then several boys casually sauntered over to where I was sitting to get a better look at the stranger. After the girl had satisfied herself that I looked harmless, some of the other children followed and began to ask me all sorts of questions in Tigrinya. The moment they realized that I hadn't understood a word of what they said, they switched to the conversational English they were learning in the classroom: "What are you called?" ... "What's your country?" ... "Do you have a wife?" ... "What's her name?" ... "How many children do you have?" ... and so on.

Then a few of the braver children climbed into my lap and gently touched my face to check on my facial hair. Although my arms aren't particularly hairy, the children were fascinated by the hairs on my arm and gently pulled on a few to make sure that they were securely attached. After about ten minutes of such horseplay, they went back to their mud castles and soccer game while a new delegation of children went through the same routine. Everyone seemed to be having a splendid time. And there was none of the desperate clutching that I had experienced upon my first visit to Solomuna. When it was time for lunch, a counselor rang a bell, and the children ran into the house because Sunday lunch was special.

As soon as they had disappeared, an old man who had been sitting on a bench next door and watching these antics came over and asked if he might join me. He was obviously disturbed about something. Perhaps I had overstepped the boundaries of proper relationships between children and adult; perhaps I should have prevented them from climbing into my lap or pulling on my hairs. But that wasn't what concerned him. Rather, in his broken but entirely comprehensible English, he apologized profusely for the children's bad behavior and begged me not to hold their rudeness against them. He assured me that Eritrean children who had been raised correctly by their parents would never behave like that. I didn't know how to respond; in my opinion, their social behavior seemed be remarkably open, friendly, engaging, and mature—at least when compared to that of American children.

Perhaps the children who had spent much of their early childhood in the Solomuna orphanage, where there were no strict rules, had never been held to the social norms and boundaries of culturally appropriate social behavior that were imposed on children who were raised by their parents and their villages. But it would take a good deal more evidence to convince me either that these orphans were naughty children who had been deprived of disciplinary control from their parents or that their social openness and familiarity were clinical indicators of residual positive attachment disorder. Given that they had already lived through difficult times of trauma, deprivation, and uncertainty, perhaps these children were just more self-confident, more competent in dealing with adversity, and more socially engaged and generous than their home-reared cousins, precisely *because* they had been raised in a communal social setting with many parents and felt self-confident and at ease in the company of adults as well as children.

The Countryside Orphanage

In contrast to the Asmara Children's Home, there was an orphanage in the countryside where the staff both lived and slept, with at least one counselor permanently assigned to each dormitory. There was a separate dining hall, and all counselors and staff ate *with* the students. There was also a small first aid station, several barns, a good-sized play area, and a large truck garden where the students raised potatoes, spinach, maize, and fruits. From the age of nine, the children attended public school or a kindergarten in town; after school, they worked with the staff on the farm.

The headmaster of this orphanage had himself been a Solomuna orphan and had worked there as a child-care counselor during the war; he was appointed headmaster at this orphanage soon after independence. Built during the Ethiopian occupation, the orphanage later came under EPLF protection. The new director and most of the counselors, a nurse who supervised a small outpatient clinic, and the administrative staff were all members of the EPLF who had worked with the children in Solomuna.

Nearly all the counselors, the nurse, and sometimes even the cooks and other ancillary staff, as well as one of the older students, regularly participated in discussions about major issues affecting the children before the director made any final decision. Taking the next step toward asserting autonomous control over their lives, the students had also organized a grievance committee that straightened out minor complaints and brought serious ones to the staff for concrete action.

In addition, the students had organized their own soccer and volleyball teams and regularly competed with the town children in local sports leagues. On religious or national holidays, of which there seemed to be an endless number, the residents were encouraged to invite their schoolmates from town to join in the festivities, and the parents from town brought special holiday foods for everybody.

An old farmer now lived at the orphanage as a combination night guard, general "handyman," avuncular father figure, and friend to the students. A kind of mentor who worked closely with the children, he taught them the basics of managing a farm. Several of the older boys were cleaning the stable and grooming the four cows that supplied milk for the orphanage, but everyone seemed to understand that the actual milking was left to the farmer. He demonstrated to the students the fine art of milking cows, but reserved the actual task for himself.

Other children were tilling and weeding in the large truck garden. When I sat down with a few boys who were weeding their own plots of land in the garden, one of them presented me with a large potato as a present for my wife. Later, as I bent down to get a better look at how well some of the plantings were progressing, a young man of maybe sixteen or seventeen came over to say hello. After asking me the usual questions about my name, marital status, and country of origin, he took me by the hand and showed me a tree that he had planted in honor of his father, who was killed in the war. His tree was part of a large grove of young trees—all "martyr trees" planted in memoriam by children who had lost their parents during the war. This living monument to the fighters killed in action served as a poignant reminder that the people of Eritrea had paid a bitter price for their independence

After I paid my respects to his victory garden, the young man invited me to help him weed his vegetable garden while we chatted. Like almost all the young people I had met in other parts of the country, he asked me with obvious pride how I liked his country. After I gave him the appropriate answer, he told me that as soon as he finished school—assuming he did well—he would become a jet pilot so he could defend his country against the Ethiopian army.

I knew of no objective criterion for judging the qualities of an orphanage, but several days at this orphanage persuaded me that it possible to organize orphanages that respect the individuality of each resident while preserving the egalitarian status of members of the community and that such establishments are probably even easier to manage than bad orphanages.

Notes

1 Peter S. Jensen and Jon Shaw, "Children as Victims of War: Current Knowledge and Future Research Needs," *Journal of the American Academy of Child and Adolescent Psychiatry* 32 (July 1993): 697–708.
2 Sandra R. Kaler and B. J. Freeman, "Analysis of Environmental Deprivation: Cognitive and Social Development in Romanian Orphans," *Journal of Child Psychology and Psychiatry* 35, no. 4 (June 1994): 769.
3 John N. McCall, "Research on the Psychological Effects of Orphanage Care: A Critical Review," in *Rethinking Orphanages for the 21st Century*, ed. Richard B. McKenzie (Thousand Oaks, Calif.: Sage, 1999), 127–150.
4 Richard B. McKenzie, "Rethinking Orphanages for the 21st Century: A Search for Reform of the Nation's Child Welfare System," in McKenzie, ed., *Rethinking Orphanages*, 289–308.

· 14 ·

REUNIFICATION

Reuniting orphans with their blood relatives would eventually become the keystone of the entire orphan protection program, because it was culturally appropriate, sustainable, and affordable. As I noted previously, extended families had always taken it for granted that they would adopt orphaned relatives who were in urgent need of protection. When that was not possible, close friends or neighbors were usually able to fill the gap.[1] However, the number of orphans who were in urgent need of protection and family care was enormous, and potential adoptive families had been scattered over the entire country and into refugee camps of neighboring countries. Finding suitable homes and families turned out to be a huge problem in a brand new country that had almost no resources.

The first thing the MLHW had to do was conduct a countrywide search to track down extended family members (aunts, uncles, grandparents), determine the state of their physical and mental health, and assess their financial ability to take in another child. This search required ready access to sufficient sources of expensive gasoline and one of the few automobiles that could maneuver on dirt roads in rough terrain (e.g., a Land Cruiser). Despite the Eritrean Relief Association's constant efforts, enough potential host families could not be found, so the search for such families had to extend beyond Eritrea to a number of the large Sudanese refugee camps.

Once the MLHW had found a suitable host family, its local representatives would make a detailed home visit to ensure that the family was emotionally and physically able to care for an additional child and that, at least to all appearances, there was a reasonably good match between child and host parents. The prospective host families had to live in a village, town, or city where the children would have ready access to schools, health care, and the like. Whenever possible, the MLHW representatives also spoke with other families in the immediate community to ensure that they would accept the reunified host family.

Most of the time, the reunification process, although protracted, went smoothly, and the adopted children got along well with their host families. There was a flaw in the process, however, which was probably unavoidable as long as the search for relatives was so difficult and costly. Most reunified orphans had never met their host families before they were brought together and, in a few cases, there were mismatches between the adopted orphans and the host families, resulting in serious emotional conflicts. Local social workers tried their best to resolve the conflicts but, when these efforts failed, some of the children ran away and found their way back to the Asmara Children's Home. After trying several alternative remedies, the MLHW decided that these children might be better off at the orphanage, where they could at least complete their primary grade education.

But the greatest obstacle that threatened to undermine the whole reunification program was the crushing poverty that affected almost every facet of daily life after the war. Families that had taken in one or more orphaned relatives in the past were no longer able to adequately feed and shelter them along with their own children, so they appealed to the MLHW to return the children to the orphanages. To prevent the reinstitutionalization of these orphans and to strengthen the practice already encoded in traditional patterns of adoption, the MLHW offered the poorest host families a monthly allowance, which was quite modest even by Eritrean standards.

But paying the poorest of the potential host families a monthly cash stipend turned out to have negative consequences. Although the payments were intended only for the neediest families, it didn't take long before relatively well-off host families (by Eritrean standards) lied about their financial status so that they too could receive cash compensation. These families began to neglect their primary means of earning a living, choosing instead to live on the dole. Moreover, since even these modest stipends made a significant difference in the lifestyle of poor families, the paternal and maternal branches of the extended families began to quarrel about which side had the legal right to take in the orphan—and thus collect the monthly stipend.

Eventually, the cash stipend scheme had to be abandoned. In its place, the MLHW instituted an income-generating plan, whereby host families could choose, for example, whether they wanted a cow for milk, a donkey for transport, a few goats for breeding, basic agricultural tools to make farming easier, or the necessary materials to open a small retail business. Committees made up of elected village representatives, MLHW representatives, and the beneficiaries themselves decided whether the income-generating assets the family had chosen were likely to generate enough income to make the family self-sufficient. They then monitored the activities of the beneficiaries and instituted explicit guidelines to ensure that the asset was used for its intended purpose and not sold for cash on the black market.[2]

Village committees also monitored the "handing over" process by which the host families received their assets: two independent witnesses countersigned every financial transaction. In collaboration with the MLHW, these committees conducted periodic workshops to inform the community about the special social problems of the orphans and their adoptive families. Legal penalties were imposed on families that gave false information. With these explicit rules and regulations, the MLHW was able to protect the reunification process from petty corruption.

By 1996, seven thousand registered orphans had been reunified; in four years, which included the second war with Ethiopia, that number had doubled; and by 2004, forty thousand orphans had been reunified with about eighteen thousand host families.[3] Although the MLHW regularly exceeded its annual "quota" of children to be reunited with their extended families, it still could not keep up with the number of newly discovered orphans who surfaced in the towns and cities of Eritrea, having returned home from refugee camps in Sudan, Ethiopia, and elsewhere.

To get a more general impression of how well the orphans fared once they were reunited with members of their extended family, Gere and I visited families in the countryside and villages whenever a ministry car and sufficient fuel were available to make the trip. Before each visit, an MLHW representative alerted the families that we might be coming to ensure that their rights to privacy were respected.

En route to one such visit, we saw no road or street signs, and most of the neighbors didn't know where the family that we were searching for lived. After following endless goat trails and repeatedly asking for directions, we finally reached a host family consisting of the host mother, her own twelve-year-old son and nine-year-old daughter, and a niece whose mother had been killed in an air raid. The woman, whose husband had died some years earlier from tuberculosis, had requested a cow as her income-generating asset, and that turned out to have been a profitable choice. The cow produced enough milk so that she could sell half of it to the neighbors and still have enough left over for the whole family. With the help of a breeding bull in the neighborhood who was periodically pressed into service, the cow had by now calved several times. The woman planned to sell several of the heifers and, at the same time, increase the production of milk she could sell.

The host mother's own two children were healthy and doing well in the local school. They both helped her with the chores after school, taking the cows to pasture, milking them at least twice a day, and selling the excess milk in the village market. Although there was always more work to do on the farm than the family could manage, the mother insisted that the best thing she could do for her children was to make sure they got a good education. As in all the other reunified families we visited, the mother in this family stuck to her agreement never to keep any of her children out of school even when they were needed to help out at home.

Throughout our visit, the niece who had been taken in was hiding behind a barn door, sometimes coming out for a quick look to see what we were up to but quickly hiding behind the barn door again. During our entire visit, the girl never spoke a word to anyone. The mother thought that the girl was either very shy or afraid that we had come to take her away; she had been concerned enough about the girl's welfare to take her to a local clinic several times. But the child was found to be neither mute nor autistic nor mentally handicapped. Although no one was ever able to say what, if anything, was wrong with her or what should be done to help her overcome her shyness, the MLHW representative made a note to check up on her in a few months. The neighbors who knew that she was an orphan agreed that she was a little strange, but the neighborhood children quickly accepted her as one of them, and most of the time she got along well with them. She was usually at the head of her class and was sometimes singled out by the teacher as a model student.

For a broader perspective on the scope of the reunification program, Gere and I spent several mornings in the Asmara Market Place speaking with vendors to assess whether they were becoming economically self-sufficient—an internal measure of the program's success. Before the war, virtually all Eritreans either farmed or managed these small stores, offering cooking oil, matches, small packets of Kleenex tissues, laundry soap, dried beans, small dishes, and small cups for the daily coffee ceremony with neither oversight nor assistance from the government. After the war, the poorest families lacked the funds necessary to rent or own store space, so, in an effort to promote financial independence, the municipal government of Asmara reserved a large area for all licensed vendors to set up small retail stores, a common sight throughout Sub-Saharan Africa. The MLHW also offered host families broader business opportunities and supported private enterprise, but we learned that few families were willing to embark on risky business ventures with which they were unfamiliar. Instead, most were inclined to take either a government-offered cow for milk, which both nourished the family and was shared with neighbors, or the goods necessary to set up one of these small stores. The shop owners generally considered the program to be a success.

Because most men of draft age were in the army, had managed to escape from Eritrea, or had already been killed, virtually all these little stores were managed by women—mostly older women who were beyond draft age. Although reluctant to leave the villages where they had lived all their lives, where they were familiar with their surroundings and felt safe, these women had all decided to settle their families in the center of Asmara, under the protection of the Ministry of Education. As to why the vast majority of reunification families had chosen to settle here, given that the competition was so stiff, the reason was always the same: as long as they earned enough money to feed and clothe their children and send them to school in clean uniforms, they all wanted to stay where the best schools in all of Eritrea were. They dreamt, however, of the day when they could return to their villages—their real homes.

The MLHW official who accompanied us on these excursions explained that these small shops were the only kind of stores that most Eritreans had ever known. Like farmers throughout the world, the host families had taken the conservative road and chosen the kinds of income-generating assets with which they had always been familiar, even if they generated only meager profits. There were, however, some adventurous families who tried to exercise their imagination. One enterprising older woman had requested a donkey, which she trained as a taxi service to carry sacks of grain or heavy packages as well as people with disabilities. Charging by the kilometer and the kilo, she used the profits she made to buy a saddle, which not only made the ride on the back of the donkey more comfortable but also allowed her to raise her prices. Everyone suspected that by now she must be wealthy, but no one ever molested her. Another host mother opened a beauty salon, which earned her a good income. But again, the vast majority of the reunification families stuck close to things that were familiar to them.

The first small retail store we visited in the Asmara Market Place was managed by a sixty-five-year-old woman who had adopted her two granddaughters several years after their parents had been killed during a firefight in a far-off village. The children, now six and ten years of age, had been listed as missing until an MLHW social worker discovered them by chance and was able to locate their grandmother, their only surviving relative, who had long ago made peace with the likelihood that the girls were dead. Once they were reunited and all the proper papers had been signed, she moved her family to Asmara, accepting the economic hardships so that her grandchildren would get a good education—for her, the highest priority. If the concerns of one generation for the next are indeed a measure of how well Eritrea would survive and prosper, the prospects for Eritrea's future seemed bright.

At first, the girls took turns waiting on customers while their grandmother watched. But, after seeing that the girls were competent and responsible, she didn't interfere and the girls gained in self-confidence. To see how well they managed, I bought a small packet of Kleenex. The younger girl took charge, made the sale correctly, and giggled as she gave me the right change while the grandmother watched proudly.

When I asked the grandmother if she could tell us a little more about her grandchildren's history, she deferred to the girls, pointing out that it was their story and they should tell it. As the older girl recounted it, their village had been a wonderful place, and they had had many friends. But then the Ethiopian soldiers raided it and forced her and her sister to watch while they shot the parents. As she got to the painful part of her story, she choked up. With Gere's help I tried to tell her that there was no need for her to go on, but she insisted; she wanted to tell her story, and her grandmother, who respected her wishes, didn't interfere.

Both sisters now liked it here in Asmara, where the schools were so much better than in their village. They made it a habit to do their homework right after school so they could help their grandmother in the store. They loved their grandmother a lot. "She always prepares good food. She buys us good clothes to wear in school. At night she checks our homework to make sure we are doing well in our studies. When I grow up, I want to become a teacher so I can support Grandmother. But I will never forget my village. One day, when I have enough money, I want to take Grandmother and my sister back to our village to show them what a nice place it was." When I last visited the family at their stall several years later, all three were still living in Asmara, and both girls were in secondary school. When Gere asked them what they wanted to do when they grew up, both repeated that they wanted to get good jobs as teachers so they could take care of their grandmother when she got old and couldn't work any longer.

There was nothing special about the next retail store we visited. Its inventory of staples was almost exactly the same as those in every other retail store in the marketplace. There was, however, something very special about the storekeeper herself—a handsome, twenty-four-year-old dynamo who exuded such self-confidence that she inspired the same in the shopkeepers around her. When Gere asked her about her experience, she told us her story in a totally matter-of-fact, even objective tone, without the slightest hesitation or complaint.

She was the oldest in a family of seven children who had grown up in a village not far from Asmara. When she was sixteen, she had been forced to watch while Ethiopian soldiers butchered both of her parents and left her with the responsibility of raising her six orphaned siblings, including a one-year-old infant. She knew that if she didn't act quickly to make a good home for them, her brothers and sisters, who were all younger than she, would end up in an orphanage, an outcome that she found totally unacceptable. So she assumed full responsibility for the care and schooling of her siblings until she heard about the MLHW reunification program and submitted her application for financial aid.

The MLHW representatives later told us that this young woman had been a brilliant student who had already been promised a place at the University of Asmara when her parents were murdered. That was the end of her academic career. She brought all six of her siblings to Asmara, where she hoped to earn enough to support them and where, like the other reunified families in Asmara, she believed her siblings had the best chance of getting a good education and good jobs after graduation, even if she had to give up her own dream of going to the university.

In her application under the program, she, like so many other reunification families, had requested the basic materials for setting up a retail shop in the central market, selling matches and cooking oil. Despite the cutthroat competition, she was always somehow able to earn enough money to feed her siblings, provide them with a safe place to live, and buy them two sets of school uniforms each. She also managed to check their homework every night so that no one would fall behind in classwork. As inflation got steadily worse throughout Eritrea, she had to take a night job while making sure that all her siblings at least finished high school—and that her brothers were working hard in school and staying out of trouble when she wasn't at home. The next-oldest sister was now studying at the university, while her two other sisters, who had graduated from high school, were helping her support the family. All this she recited without any complaints and with a pragmatic attitude, as if she had analyzed her situation carefully. I had no idea how she did it, but from her demeanor and cheerful interaction with the other shopkeepers, she was clearly doing it and doing it well.

With what must have been an infinite reserve of good will, good cheer, and healthy skepticism, as if she were challenging the world to defeat her, she remained convinced that she would prevail. When I asked if she had ever thought about going back to school, she stared at me for a moment and then burst out laughing, assuring me that filling up her spare time was the least of her worries. My question must have sounded as idiotic to her as it probably would have to billions of women throughout the world who spend twenty-five hours a day feeding their families while trying to keep body and soul together.

As we were about to leave, she gave us a cheery salute and turned to the next customer, who was probably wondering why I was asking such stupid questions. Once we had said our goodbyes and arranged for further home visits over the next few days, I realized that my brief encounter with this young woman had left me totally disoriented, embarrassed, and confused about my own station in life. Thanks to her Herculean efforts, this young woman and her siblings didn't belong to the "absolutely poor," who go to sleep every night still hungry and lack access to any kind of medical care, safe drinking water, or sanitary facilities. What threw me so completely off track was the realization that I had never in my life *felt* what more than three-quarters of the world's population experience every day—what it means to know in your bones that you were born poor, that you will always be poor, that you will die poor, and that every dreary day will be exactly like the last one. It's hard to imagine having to face that reality and not giving in to despair.

But that extraordinary young woman couldn't afford to give in to despair. What seemed to keep her alive was her indomitable good spirits and her determination to see all her siblings graduate from secondary school. She must have resolved that she would "never kneel down." If given half a chance for peace, the next generation of Eritreans might still salvage their future. Perhaps she would never storm the barricades for the revolution, but she was making it possible for all her siblings to turn the dream of universal literacy into a reality. Long after we had left the market area, that moment of clarity became for me the essence of the entire independence struggle that would have to continue long after the shooting stopped.

Notes

1 Morah, Mebrathu, and Sebhatu, "Evaluation of the Orphan Reunification Project."
2 See, for example, Morah, Mebrathu, and Sebhatu, "Evaluation of the Orphan Reunification Project in Eritrea"; and Ministry of Labour and Human Welfare (MLHW), *Impact Assessment of the Orphan Reunification Project* (Asmara, Eritrea: Government of the State of Eritrea, 1998).
3 MLHW, *Impact Assessment of the Orphan Reunification Project.*

· 15 ·

GROUP HOMES

In their overall plan for the rescue and rehabilitation of more than ten thousand orphans, Assefaw and his colleagues had made allowance for the likelihood that there would a small group of children who probably had no living relatives anywhere in Eritrea and had no place to go. These were the most vulnerable of all the vulnerable children, who might be doomed to spend the rest of childhood in some kind of orphanage unless the MLHW could find an alternative.

To close that gap, they included plans for a network of small group homes in strategic locations throughout country, where all orphaned children would have a home of their own even though they had no extended family to provide for their care, protection, and education. These homes were to be constructed on the periphery of large towns, where the orphans would have ready access to schools, health-care facilities, and cultural activities. Further, they would be built in a style that blended in with the other houses in the neighborhood and would not be readily identifiable as the place where the orphans lived.

The chronic shortages of building materials, architects, and contractors made progress slower than expected. At the outset, in the mid-1990s, there were three group homes, and the construction of additional group homes was delayed for several years. By 2009, twenty-two homes were in operation throughout the country, providing shelter for a total of 270 orphans.

The group homes were kept small, housing at most twelve children of different ages, one permanently assigned live-in housemother, and one assistant housemother who helped with the daily chores but went home at night. Each group home had three bedrooms for the children, each of which was furnished with two bunk beds and adequate closet space for the children to keep their personal belongings. Housemothers had their own private bedrooms, but were always available in case a child had a bad scare in the middle of the night. Each group home also had a large modern kitchen equipped with a conventional *injera* stove for the traditional large pancakes; two bathrooms with toilets; a storeroom; and one large common room where residents ate their meals, did their homework, socialized, and were allowed to watch one hour a day of "appropriate" television. Most of the homes were built on large plots of land enclosed by stone walls; here, the children could play ball and were encouraged to grow their own vegetables and flowers and to plant trees that would one day offer the next generation of orphans shade in the hot sun.

Selection committees chosen by the village council held workshops to educate the community at large about the needs of these children. They ensured that the orphans were treated with kindness and respect, and they monitored the children's emotional and physical health. Serious psychological or social difficulties were reported to the MLHW representative, who made whatever adjustments could be made in the lives of the children.

Before taking up their duties, housemothers-in-training attended a series of workshops on child development and then spent a few months with one of the established housemothers for a kind of "in-service" training. The arrangement also gave established housemothers a chance to observe how prospective housemothers interacted with the children.

With the help of an MLHW representative who made sure that everything went smoothly, Gere and I regularly visited several of the group homes in different parts of the country to monitor the orphans' progress, their emotional well-being, and their social integration into the community. On one of our unscheduled visits, two older girls had gone into town with their housemother so she could show them how to shop and bargain for lower prices. The assistant housemother was preparing lunch, and some of the children were doing their homework in the dining room while others were just returning from school. With great dignity and all the appropriate ceremonial gestures reserved for honored guests, one of the girls served us tea and sweet bread while we waited for the housemother to return from the market.

When the housemother came home with the girls, she told us about the history of the children, their behavior when they first came to the home, and the course of their recovery and development. Most of the children had cried a lot when they first arrived. During the early months, some wet their beds and fought with other children.

Snapshots

Fiori had come to the group home with her younger brother when she was ten. She had an older sister who was still living in the Asmara Orphanage.

> "I remember almost nothing about my past; I don't remember how I got to this place [the group home]. They told me my father was killed in the war and my mother died after being sick for a long time. When my parents died, someone brought me to my uncle, who was also a fighter, but he couldn't take care of me, so he took me to the orphanage when I was five. I was very unhappy in that place. Some of the mothers [caregivers] beat me when I didn't do what they told us to do; the older children beat and bullied me. As soon as I came here, everything got better. The [house] mother here has always been kind to me; she makes me feel that someone wants me. When I'm sad and want to cry, she listens to me. The other children are all my friends."

Fiori still has frequent nightmares and wets her bed at night.

> "Sometimes I think about my sister in the orphanage and then I can't stop crying, but I'm now doing much better in school. If only my sister could come here and live with us as a family, life would be better. When I'm grown up, I want to become a teacher and help our mother."

After six months of repeated appeals to the MLHW, the housemother finally succeeded in bringing Fiori's older sister to the group home. Since then, when assigning orphans to group homes, the MLHW has arranged to keep one space vacant in case a lost sibling is found.

Salina, age thirteen, was the oldest surviving member of her family. She now lived in the group home with her siblings Mogo, age seven, and Hariena, age nine. An Eritrean family had adopted one of the other sisters. Salina had no memories of her past and refused to talk about her life at home before she and her siblings became orphans. From the way she denied having any memories, it was clear that her memories were very dark. To make sure that I didn't push her to talk about things that were too painful, the housemother firmly intervened and requested that we not ask any more about Salina's early childhood. From time to time, Salina still had nightmares and night terrors.

Once the girl was outside watching the other children play with the dog, the housemother told us that Salina had been present when her father, who had been diagnosed as schizophrenic, killed her mother and then shot himself. No one knew whether any of the other siblings now living in the same house remembered anything about the tragedy. A nun had placed Salina and her siblings in a Catholic orphanage in Keren.

"I have good memories of my friends there and would really like to visit them again. The children all had their own beds, and I never had any trouble sleeping, even though the orphanage was always overcrowded. Thirty of us had to sleep in the same room, and the place was always so noisy that I couldn't do my lessons. [But] there was always enough food, the food was good, and the rooms were clean. The mothers were kind to all of us; there was a nice playground; everyone worked and played together. It was as if I was still living in my village. Sometimes the children got into arguments, but then they settled the problem all by themselves and the mothers never interfered. The older ones helped younger children. My older brother is now working somewhere on his own, but when I was small he always helped me. Now I do the same for my younger brother and sister. I try to help all the younger children here with their studies or when they don't keep their rooms clean.

> "But life here [in the group home] is even better; it's more organized. There is a schedule for mealtimes, for studying, for playing, and for sleeping. Mother teaches us how to prepare food, how to cook injera. She takes us to the market and shows us how to buy things for the right price, how to handle money. I'm working hard in school so that I can become a teacher so I can support my mother."

The steady improvement in the children's social and academic behavior and the five prizes for academic excellence displayed on the wall of the common room attested to the housemother's success in encouraging the children to work hard in school so they would get good jobs when they grew up. She had mounted the five school prizes on the wall so that the other children could see how hard their brothers and sisters were working in school. Whenever a child lagged behind, she visited the schoolteachers to find out how she could help the child improve and requested supplementary teaching materials.

While the housemother chatted with us, two boys swept the floor and set the table while three of the older girls helped the assistant housemother prepare the noon meal of the traditional *injera* pancake, which was covered with *shiro* (chickpeas) and spicy sauce from the communal platter. With the satisfaction of a mother hen, the housemother briefly glanced at what the children were doing and saw no need to interfere. The children then sat down together at the dining table, with the oldest girl making sure that Tarik, the youngest boy, was able to climb into his chair. Before anyone started eating, the oldest boy said a traditional Coptic prayer, and the others solemnly folded their hands. I assumed it was the housemother, a Coptic Christian, who had encouraged the children to pray before meals, but I didn't ask.

After saying their prayers with great solemnity (and occasional giggling when they saw that I was watching), they dug into their lunch with gusto. To make sure that Tarik got his share of the meal, the oldest girl put some of the pancake aside in a secluded corner of the platter, an allocation that everybody acknowledged and respected. From sweeping the floor to setting the table, from helping to cook the *injera*, adding hot peppers and green vegetables, to laying out the food and sharing it from a communal platter, the whole meal proceeded without a hint of regimentation or the need for any kind of assistance from the housemother. Like their elders, the children had elevated eating to an important social function.

When the whole gang was outside, the oldest girl took the fruit and cookies that Gere had brought and divided them into equal portions so that everybody, including me, got a fair share. While we were finishing our orange slices in the yard, a young puppy suddenly appeared from out of nowhere, licked the children's faces, wagged his tail furiously, and barked until the children agreed to chase him around the yard. Coming across a healthy young dog in Eritrea who was not afraid of people and of whom the children were not afraid—who instead seemed to be a member of the family—came as a total surprise to me. The only dogs I had ever encountered in that country were either guard dogs who snarled, bared their teeth, and would probably bite any stranger who came close, or flea-bitten mongrels who cowered in terror whenever any human being was near. My encounter with this jolly puppy was entirely different. The housemother had bought the puppy from neighbors so that the children would have a companion who loved them unconditionally. With her help, the older children had formed a trusting relationship with the dog and were not in the least afraid.

As a dog fancier myself, I felt included when the puppy cuddled up next to me on the steps and the children formed a circle around us so that they could satisfy their curiosity about me. Like the children at the Comboni School, first they inspected the hairs on my arms, carefully pulling on one or two to test whether they were firmly attached. Then they began to interview me. Using classroom English, they asked the usual questions about my name, my home, whether I was married, how many children I had, and what I did for work. Then they told me about their plans for the future. Most had their hearts set on becoming teachers, two planned to become doctors, two hoped to become professional soccer players, and one boy, like so many others I encountered, couldn't wait to become a jet pilot.

After we had exchanged biographical sketches and the puppy had wandered off to find a shady place to nap, the youngest girl, who had been waiting impatiently, boldly took me by the hand, dragged me to a young papaya tree in the backyard, and through an elaborate set of gestures explained that this was her tree. She had planted it and now watered it every day. She further explained that the papaya fruits weren't ready to be eaten yet, but when they were ripe, everybody would share.

Each of the other children then went through the same routine. Without shuffling or pushing, they patiently lined up in a row, then, one by one, took me by the hand and dragged me to their papaya trees for a photograph. Once everybody had been photographed with her or his tree, the young girl made a full sweeping gesture with her arm, pointed to my camera, and made it perfectly clear in local sign language that she wanted me to take a group picture of everyone, with the housemother in the middle.

When the photography shoot was finished, the housemother took me aside and, with Gere's help, explained that foreign visitors often came to see the children and almost always took a few photographs. But when the photo sessions were over, they almost always got into their cars and went home, and the children never saw the photos. That's all she needed to say; she had made her point perfectly clear. With Gere's help, I managed to send a full set of photographs—one picture for each child together with his or her tree, and a group picture of the children with their housemother. When I returned a year later to check on whether the papayas were ripe, the girl who had engineered the photography session pulled me to a large poster board on the wall of the common room, where the housemother had mounted the pictures. She pointed first to herself and then to her picture to make sure that I understood it was the same person; then, with a grand sweep of both arms, she indicated that the other pictures were of the other kids in the group home.

Had I grown up in Eritrea and observed how mothers interact with their own, biological children, I would probably have concluded that these children had been spoiled by their parents (and, incidentally, that I had been far too permissive), that they had been much too familiar and failed to respect the boundaries separating children and adults, and that their behavior was clearly an indication of their severe deprivation in early childhood and symptomatic of a positive attachment disorder. Had the old man who watched our horseplay at the Comboni School been right, after all? Were these children being naughty because of a lack of proper upbringing, or were they acting "out of control" because they couldn't contain their hunger for affection? Perhaps I had taken the behavior of the Eritrean orphans too much at face value. Yet nothing in their behavior could have convinced me that they were anything but open, trusting, friendly, and good-natured—very likely more so than home-reared children. Obviously sensitive to the feelings of others, they were willing to help other children. Perhaps, during their early years in the base camps, these children had absorbed the same experience-based values as the EPLF—including, for example, egalitarianism—and their behavior reflected the EPLF subculture and ideology rather than the neurotic behavior of deprived, frustrated, overly forward children who were at odds with the traditionally reserved ("inhibited"), respectful social behavior expected of young children in the presence of adults. At least so it seemed to me after watching the social interaction between children, housemother, and puppy. In clinical terminology, in other words, the children were *not* suffering from an attachment disorder. Quite to the contrary, and at the risk of overinterpreting disconnected clinical indicators, I believe they had internalized an egalitarian perspective on human social relationships that diminished the emotional distance between adults and children, or between teacher and students. They were, in essence, "securely attached."

All the housemothers whom we interviewed were illiterate, but they all seemed to have an innate knack for doing exactly the right and culturally appropriate thing at the right time to bring a troubled child back from the edge of despair. They intuitively knew not to interfere if they believed a child was capable of working out a problem on his or her own. Whatever the source of their implicit knowledge, it seemed to me that they presented an invaluable resource of folk-knowledge for prospective new housemothers and might even be able to give Western child-care specialists a fresh perspective on best practices in child care.

After checking with Gere to make sure that I wasn't being intrusive, I asked the housemother, whom we had often visited, whether she would tell me a little about her experiences, which could be of great help to future housemothers. She was visibly pleased to be asked and fully competent to describe in detail what she thought every housemother should know to be up to the task. Before going into any detail, she emphasized, as a kind of preamble, that every caregiver must always remember that these children had suffered a great deal before coming to the group home and that, no matter what a housemother might do, it would take them some time before they felt comfortable and accepted in their new social setting. She had found that imposing discipline—scolding or punishing them for misbehaving, fighting, stealing, lying, and the like—was a waste of time and effort. It certainly didn't help and, given that this was often the time when the children were most vulnerable, most miserable, least trusting, and most difficult to manage, it could actually make them more belligerent and withdrawn. Instead, she gave them as much love and support as she could to make them feel wanted. After six to twelve months, most of the children started to feel at home. They began to get along better with the others, join in group activities, and do much better in school. Most important, they no longer looked upon the future as hopeless

When the children were confronted by everyday problems, she believed that it was essential to let them struggle on their own to find solutions rather than rely on predigested answers. In this respect, I had the impression that the housemother was following the lesson plan that Beraki had already gleaned from Piaget's pedagogical methods—namely, to integrate theory and praxis.

When new children first came to a group home (she continued), prospective housemothers should make it clear that everyone was expected to work together to keep the house and its surroundings clean, prepare meals, and water their trees. The older children were expected to help the younger ones with difficult tasks, but were always to give them a chance to see whether they could do the tasks by themselves.

But, in her estimation, the most important advice she could give any potential housemothers was that they had to restore the children's trust. Otherwise, everything else would be a waste of time. And if the housemother expected the children to trust her, she must first show that she trusted them. For example, she told us that the children sometimes asked her for a few pennies so that they could go to a local shop to buy a trinket or sweet. They knew that if their request was modest, she would give them the money. She always left her purse on the table in plain sight, where they could easily have stolen money. But as far as she knew, none of the children had ever taken a penny without asking first.

Had she locked up the purse, the children would sense that she didn't trust them, and that would make it difficult for them to trust her. But once they were convinced that she trusted them, they began to trust her. From that point on, their behavior also improved dramatically. It was as if trust were the key to their emotional recovery.

The experiences of young Tarik convinced me that such group homes might be an optimal setting for rescuing and rehabilitating orphans who had no other options. Tarik had been raised in a large, church-sponsored institution since infancy, but was then transferred to the group home, where he had been living for several months when I first met him. The moment I sat down in the common room, he took me by the hand, pulled me into his bedroom, and proudly showed me a crib with side railings that had been prepared especially for him so that he wouldn't fall out of bed at night. I had no idea what was so special about his bed until the housemother told us Tarik's story.

When Tarik was only four, the MLHW had decided to remove him from the church-sponsored orphanage to one of the small group homes where there was a vacancy, even though MLHW regulations specified that orphans had to be at least five years old for such a placement. Once safely settled in the group home, Tarik, a soft-spoken and agreeable child, adjusted well. The other children liked him almost immediately, treated him like the baby brother of the family, looked out for his special needs, and helped him however they could while also encouraging him to be self-reliant.

After he had lived in the group home for almost a half year and had become an integral part of the family, some administrative MLHW bureaucrat decided that Tarik should be returned to the orphanage. Given how much Tarik already meant to the other children, the housemother knew that she had to be straightforward with them, so she called a general meeting to give the children the bad news. As soon as she finished her announcement, there was a small-scale revolution. Outraged, the children loudly protested that Tarik was their brother and that no one had the right to take him away. And they threatened that if he were taken way, they would go on strike and refuse to go to school.

Tarik himself, upon hearing about the plan, screamed, stamped his feet, and insisted that this was his home, that the housemother was his mother, and that he would run away if forced to go back to the orphanage. For three days, the children agitated on his behalf and risked getting bad marks in class by staying out of school. After they marched in protest on the nearby town of Mendefera, they eventually persuaded the MLHW representative to reverse the decision and restore Tarik to his rightful place in the family. For Tarik, the bed represented special treatment, and in his four year old head, that meant *he* was special.

The children had learned the important lesson: that it is possible not only to question authority at the grassroots but sometimes even to challenge and defeat it when that authority threatens to deny them their basic human rights. The last time I visited the group home, Tarik was his cheerful, self-confident, and socially engaged self again.

· 1 6 ·

EDUCATION AFTER LIBERATION

In precolonial Eritrea, just as in most former colonial territories of Africa, there were no officially recognized organized schools in the villages, towns, and cities. Only a handful of children had ever received any formal education, and that education was almost exclusively in Coptic Christian seminaries or Koranic madrassas. When the Italian expeditionary forces occupied Eritrea, they opened two- and four-year elementary schools that would serve the colonial administration by training interpreters, domestic servants, factory workers, agricultural laborers, typists, and seamstresses. By order of the fascist Italian government, no Eritrean was allowed to advance beyond the fifth grade and, after 1936, no one was allowed to rise beyond the *third* grade.[1] Apart from the Scuola Vittoria Emmanuel in Asmara, only six of the twenty-five schools for Eritreans provided basic literacy and vocational training up to fourth grade. The Scuola Salvago Ruggio in Keren offered two-year courses for children of some privileged Eritreans, or *balabats*.

After the British defeated the Italian occupation army early in 1941, they built many elementary schools, a few middle schools, and two secondary schools. They hired teachers who were fluent in Tigrinya, English, and Arabic and, using a traditional curriculum, they taught the children reading and writing as well as the fundamentals of agriculture, carpentry, other cottage industries, and home economics. Then, after World War II, when the UN mandated the federation of Eritrea with Ethiopia, Haile Selassie imposed Amharic, the official language of Ethiopia, in all Eritrean classrooms, to the exclusion of Tigrinya, and ordered that all books written in Tigrinya be burned. Thus, until the liberation of Eritrea in 1991–1993, the official languages taught to Eritrea's children had long been foreign.

The Language Question

With liberation came the hotly debated question of what should be the official language of government as well as of instruction in independent Eritrea, a small country where the large majority of the population spoke one of two major languages (Tigray as well as Tigrinya) and the remaining population, all minorities, spoke their own indigenous languages.

In the base camps, combatants, peasants, parents, and teachers already had strongly supported the policy that English would be the official language of instruction for all Eritrean students above the fifth grade. But in the early 2000s, the government mandated that all children be taught in their mother tongue (Afar, Bilen, Nara, Hdareb, Kunama, Rashaida, and Saho) for the first five school grades in order to reinforce the cultural identity of the different nationalities. This mandate met with strong opposition. The parents in the minority communities argued that the number of children and adults, let alone teachers, who spoke any of the seven minority languages was very small. Moreover, teaching the children in their mother tongues would make it harder for them to develop a sense of national unity across cultural differences. More importantly, it would deny them the linguistic tools for direct access to the outside world of science, technology, and commerce. In short, it would prevent them from being able to communicate with the world community and would put them at a great social and intellectual disadvantage, as if they were strangers in a foreign country. These parents therefore joined forces with the thousands of families returning from Sudanese refugee camps, where they had begun to speak Arabic, and they all demanded that their children be taught in either Arabic or Tigrinya through fifth grade, not in their mother tongue. But Arabic was also opposed by the government.

Although never explicitly stated in such bald terms, the language of instruction for children in the first five grades was obviously a hot political rather than educational issue. Isaias Afwerki's objection to Arabic as the mother tongue was probably a xenophobic reaction, reflecting a concern that if Muslim children were taught in Arabic during their earliest and most impressionable years, the Muslim population would eventually displace Coptic Christians as the dominant political, religious, and ideological majority in Eritrea. The parents persuasively argued that Arabic is a world language of cross-border commerce and is therefore far more useful for communication throughout many regions of Africa, the Middle East, and parts of Southeast Asia than their obscure languages. But the president rejected all deviations from his mandate.

The Choice of Curriculum

Under the 1989 "United Nations Convention of the Rights of the Child," all children became entitled by law to an elementary education. Having won the war for independence from Ethiopia, the Eritreans now had to secure a stable and functioning society, and nowhere was this more important than in the area of education, where they faced enormous demands for universal literacy. At least twenty-seven thousand Eritrean students who had been going to school in the liberated areas of their occupied land were now waiting to continue their education in independent Eritrea.

Wherever we traveled throughout the country, we saw new school buildings being built. But ten years after liberation, despite such impressive activity, there were never enough schools for all the elementary school children, let alone enough teachers, chairs, desks, blackboards, and school supplies. Moreover, there was only about a third of the teachers and classrooms needed to accommodate all secondary grade students, and, at most, a quarter of the teachers and classrooms needed to help aspiring teachers realize their hope of enrolling in the University of Asmara once they had completed their twelve years of formal education.

With up to sixty students in one classroom, overcrowding was a critical problem, and parents began to object. One strategy for combating this problem was to divide the school day into morning and afternoon sessions. Twice as many children were now able to go to school and learn from direct contact with the teachers, although the teachers were now able to devote even less time to individual students.

However, after thirty years of unrelenting warfare, another problem facing the provisional government was the formulation of a curriculum specifically designed for Eritrea's children, who had lived through very hard times. Should the government try to resurrect and expand integrated "theory and praxis," the entirely new and progressive curriculum to which Beraki and his research team had devoted so many years at the Zero School? Would such an educational philosophy, which was designed to prepare students to safeguard, strengthen, and enlarge the major pillars of Eritrea's continuing struggle for freedom, be viable in peacetime?

Undoubtedly, a Socratic dialogue reinforced by ad hoc experimental demonstrations was the ideal that, from all available evidence, had been achieved at the Zero School. But while this curriculum had worked so well in the base camps, where there were totally committed teachers inspired by a rational approach to democratic teaching and learning, it was much too complex and labor-intensive to be implemented in the classroom during the early postwar years, when there was a critical shortage of teachers, schools, classrooms, and teaching materials, when hundreds of thousands of children were impatiently clamoring to go to school, and when so much would have to be done in a very short time. It was also much too cumbersome to assess, should the Ministry of Education insist on annual quantitative evaluations.

Given all the material and human resources that were available throughout liberated Eritrea, it would be much easier to train new teachers in—and, at least by some criteria, to assess the effects of—a curriculum that would be more cost-effective in teaching large groups of children the mechanics of reading and writing, without any concern for how they used language to create meanings, question authority, and make change. Rather than creating opportunities for one-on-one dialogues with individual students to encourage problem solving and critical thinking, the circumstances favored behavior modification and contingent reinforcement, the labor-saving methods of drill-and-rote learning. Thus, by 2004 or 2005, an entirely new curriculum—one based on rote learning and memorization—had been assembled under government pressure.

This new curriculum soon became the target of withering criticism. First the parents, then the teachers, and then the ministers openly protested that far too many students were failing in school or dropping out because they were unable to meet the minimum criteria for graduation. It was critical that the Ministry of Education formulate a new educational plan as quickly as possible. By then, however, the issue of how, where, and under what conditions Eritrea's children should be taught was no longer a pedagogical one but instead a politically sensitive one, touching on fears of encroaching Arabization and the suppression of a Christian minority in Eritrea.

Some high school graduates who performed well in their examinations were able to continue their studies at Asmara University or, after the president had temporarily closed the university (fearing that the students might become the nucleus of a new rebellion against the government), at one of the newly formed technical schools. But those students who didn't make the cut on their final examinations were conscripted into the armed forces to support Isaias's useless military remobilization on the front lines. In other words, the government effectively neutralized all attempts to reform the Eritrean curriculum for Eritrean children and made sure that neither the students nor their parents would become the trigger point for mass demonstrations calling for regime change. For all intents and purposes, this was the end of serious education in Eritrea.

Note

1 Adane Taye, *A Historical Survey of State Education in Eritrea* (Asmara, Eritrea: Educational Materials Production and Distribution Agency, Ministry of Education, Republic of Eritrea, 1991), 43.

· 17 ·

COMMUNITY CHILD-CARE CENTERS

In his report to UNESCO in 1948, Piaget recommended that "kindergarten for underprivileged children should offer them ethically and intellectually stimulating surroundings in which the atmosphere and above all the abundant and diversified material employed will compensate for the shortcomings of their family life and arouse their curiosity and energies."[1]

By 2000, the World Bank and Eritrea's Education Ministry had negotiated a large loan to enable the Eritrean government to integrate separate projects of early childhood education, nutrition and public health, and orphan protection into existing preschools under a comprehensive program of Early Childhood Development. This restructuring, the World Bank believed, would greatly improve the use of resources and ultimately be more effective in addressing the needs of the youngest children.

During a field trip in early 2000 to see how well these preschools functioned, Gere and I first visited two towns in the Gash-Barka region, where the Ministry of Education had recently opened two kindergartens. The buildings themselves were light, airy, and well equipped with culturally appropriate wooden toys—blocks and jigsaw puzzles—that a skilled carpenter and his assistants had made in sufficient quantity to be distributed in local shops throughout Eritrea and abroad to help pay for teachers and building maintenance.

Educated in one of the larger teacher-training facilities in Asmara, the teachers worked well together to create an open and relaxed atmosphere that encouraged the children to organize games on their own, but they always made themselves available when the children asked for help. When the children came to school, they all changed into the same neat school uniforms for which the parents had to pay a hefty fee. When the teachers announced that it was time to go home, they hung up their uniforms on hooks with their names attached, lined up in single file, and walked home with a teacher in the lead. Our visit to the other kindergarten in a nearby town was almost identical.

The atmosphere in both kindergartens reminded me of that in well-to-do kindergartens in Western cities. For the first time in their lives, these children had ample opportunities to exercise their spirit rather than be regimented, as they were in the traditional schools. The experience no doubt opened many doors for them; if money were not always the limiting factor, all of Eritrea's children would no doubt have benefited greatly from it. But after thirty years of war, the country was bankrupt, and it was impossible for the Ministry of Education to build many such kindergartens.

The next preschool we visited was in a small village in the northern Red Sea region. All the families were Muslims and were, by conventional standards, extremely poor. Most of the inhabitants were nomads who spent half the year in their coastal villages and the other half traveling in search of grazing land for their livestock. Most spoke their mother tongue or Arabic or both, but they did not speak Tigrinya and certainly not Amharic. The villages scattered along the Red Sea coast were too small to qualify for government assistance to build a kindergarten of their own, but this community was intent on getting some kind of learning center where its children could learn how to read, and it would not be put off.

So the villagers took matters into their own hands to build their own local Community Child-Care Center (CCCC). To finance the center and support a teacher, all the families tithed themselves until they had raised enough money to buy a tent that could accommodate at least forty to fifty children huddled together on the dirt floor. They then hired a young woman with some experience looking after young children to teach the foundations of reading and writing—although no one was exactly sure how this should be done or whether it was even necessary since, given the right sociolinguistic environment for enough hours every day, most illiterate children would learn how to read and write, anyway.

When we visited that first CCCC, we entered the tent through the back door so as not to disturb the class in progress. The children had their eyes glued on the teacher, who was leading them in an exercise designed to teach the fundamentals of translating printed symbols into speech sounds. She stood facing them, holding up eight to ten large cards on which she had drawn pictures of domestic animals—a cow, a goat, a camel, a bird, a fish, and so forth—for them to identify. Sometimes she asked the class to name the animal in unison; other times she called on individual children who had raised their hands, indicating that they wanted to give a solo performance. Sometimes it was impossible to tell the difference. All the children waved their hands wildly to show that they knew the answer. This recitation wasn't exactly what Beraki would have considered critical thinking, but the children were obviously having a wonderful time showing off what they knew.

The last place we visited that day was another small fishing village that also did not qualify for the construction of a kindergarten, and the whole community had likewise pitched in to buy a large tent and hire a teacher. Here, too, the teacher relied on rote repetition to teach the children how to link the names of objects and the objects themselves, thus learning to read. The only difference was that her stimulus cards depicted Arabic letters and single-digit numbers instead of farm animals.

Given the positive impact that preschool education has been shown to have on both physical and mental development, one might have predicted that the Eritrean children who had spent a year in an established kindergarten would have a substantial advantage over those who had spent the same year matching symbols (pictures, single-digit numbers) with words in the CCCCs. But to the surprise of virtually everyone associated with school administration and educational planning, clinical observations of the two groups by Ministry of Education staff showed no significant differences in school readiness. If anything, the children who had spent a year in one of the CCCCs had a slight advantage.

If these findings could have been replicated in other towns or villages, they might have been of considerable interest to the Ministry of Education for setting policies of early childhood education. At least such a study might have motivated present and future ministers to consider the larger context in which children going to school learn not only the mechanics of reading but also the deeper process of learning to read for meaning. In such a context, children are socialized, learn on their own, and get the essential intellectual stimulation[2] that has little to do with learning the names of farm animals or numbers. But after peacetime, Eritrea largely abandoned the base camp–style of free-spirited learning.

Figure 1. Children in the Asmara orphanage taking a break from activities.

Figure 2. Teacher playing with the children in the orphanage playground.

Figure 3. Two of the combatants working in the underground electronics workshop.

Figure 4. Students planting vegetables at the Zero School – an example of "Theory and Praxis" agriculture.

Figure 5. Caregiver with children at breakfast. (Asmara Orphanage)

Figure 6. Lunchtime in the group home.

Figure 7. Several of the children sleeping in an underground cave, where they're protected from the bombing raids.

Figure 8. Students in class at the Zero School.

Figure 9. The group home mascot.

Figure 10. Friends posing for the camera. (Asmara Orphanage)

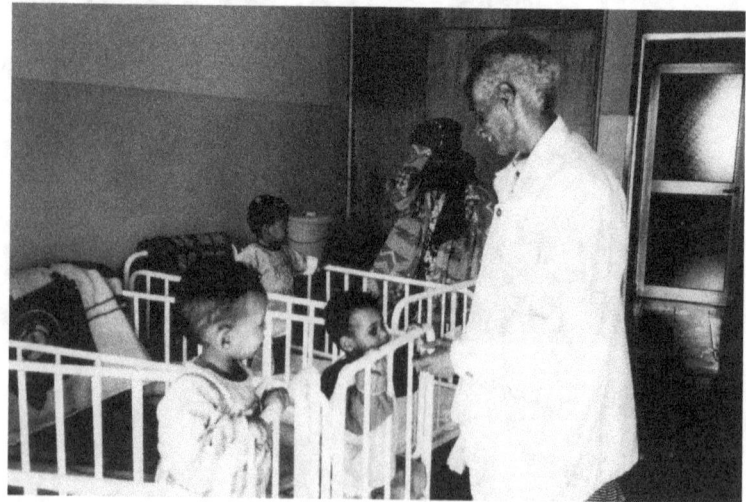

Figure 11. Asmara Orphanage

Figure 12. The house mother and Tarik after he returned to his group home.

Figure 13. Air raid.

Figure 14. Children heading off for their bath.

Figure 15. Students attending class in the Zero School.

Figure 16. Movie night under the stars.

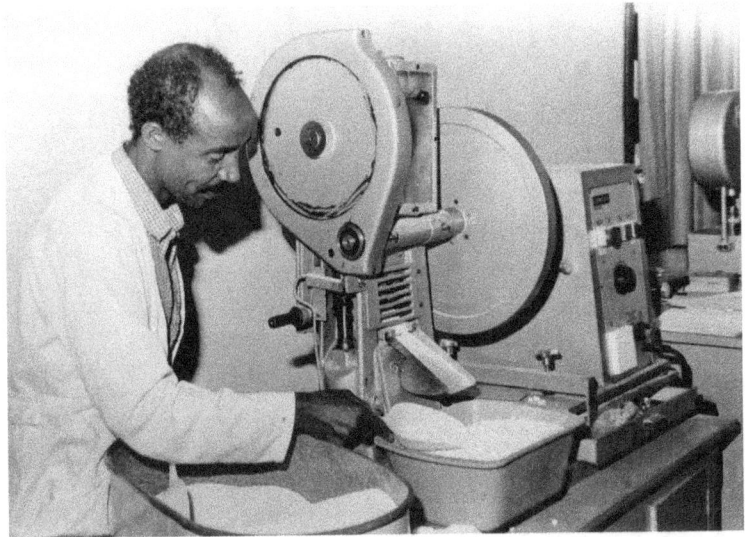

Figure 17. A snapshot of the underground pharmacy where the most essential pharmaceuticals were produced.

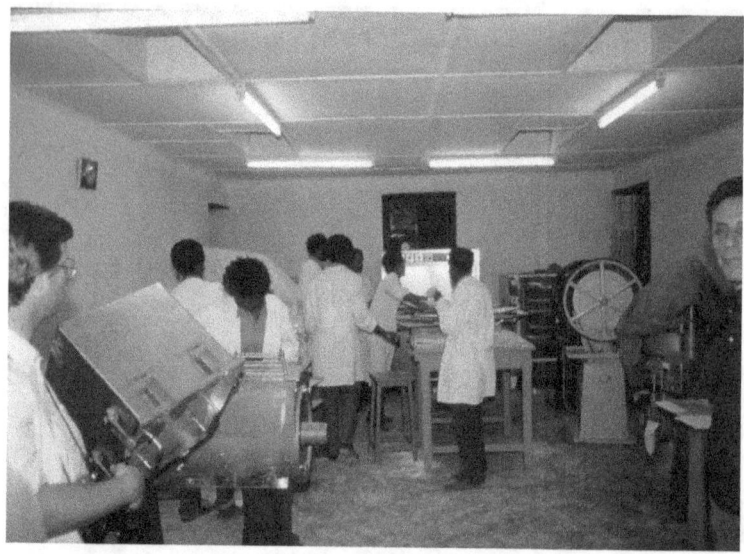

Figure 18. Producing pharmaceuticals in the underground pharmacy.

Notes

1 Piaget, *To Understand Is to Invent*, 5.
2 Piaget, *To Understand Is to Invent*.

Part III
A Dubious Liberation

· 18 ·

A NEW GOVERNMENT

Once the war ended, it took just over two years to convert the dream of a free, open, and democratic society into the nightmare of nighttime arrest and secret incarceration. Following his election in 1993, Isaias Afwerki disbanded the EPLF, replaced it with the People's Front for Democracy and Justice (PFDJ), appointed himself chairman of the new party, and prohibited the formation of any other political parties. He rescinded all civil rights and disallowed open assembly. Those ministers who objected to his policies were jailed or "disappeared," replaced by yes-men who enthusiastically supported his quirky decisions.

From the years of armed struggle under control of the EPLF to the early years of independence, grassroots organizations such as the National Union of Eritrean Women (NUEW), the National Eritrean Union of Youth and Students, the National Union of Eritrean Teachers, the Organization of Disabled Combatants, and so forth, had tried valiantly to continue functioning as independent organizations that advocated successfully for the rights of their constituents, including women, students and youth, teachers, union members, and peasants. But feeling threatened by the prospect of these grassroots organizations growing in strength and depriving him of absolute power, Isaias eliminated or neutralized them. For example, he appointed himself chairman of the NUEW and restructured its policies to further distance them from the union's original mission. His pretext was that, under the particular economic conditions in Eritrea at the time, the rights of Eritrean women had to be sacrificed for the greater good—namely, economic development (i.e., national reconstruction) and modernization in general.

Predictably, efforts to squelch potential dissent went beyond the unions. The independent village assemblies that had been organized in the field to collaborate with the EPLF to address the needs, demands, and critiques of populations in the liberated zones were essentially rendered impotent, if not completely outlawed. When Zero School graduates petitioned the government for permission to form an alumni association for those who had learned and worked at the school during the war, permission was denied. When the former and current students and graduates of Asmara University sought permission to form a students' association, Isaias finally agreed—provided that the association's officers were under his control.

How could this have happened? Had no one noticed the president's gradual assumption of dictatorial powers? How was it possible for the Eritreans—having stubbornly fought a war against an external enemy that no one believed they could defeat—to "kneel down" so easily and submit to the internal threat of a mean-spirited petty dictator. Given Eritrea's history of humiliation and repeated subjugation, it was high time to oppose this new totalitarian regime. But the people, especially the cadres and members of the president's cabinet, were afraid and kept silent.

After the newly liberated country's initial attempt at demobilization, a general remobilization was undertaken, and most of the ex-combatants were simply swept up in it. Intent on building up his military, Isaias also decreed that young people of draft age be conscripted into the armed forces for up to ten years in what would, in many cases, amount to a useless military remobilization on the front lines. There, the rank and file had nothing to do except wait for another Ethiopian assault while the generals, having too much free time on their hands, started new farms or rehabilitated old ones and put the soldiers to work for minimum wages. Pregnant women were exempt from the draft law, so many young women deliberately got pregnant to avoid military service. Others simply dropped out of school in the eleventh grade.

Meanwhile, the military leaders had settled down in the luxurious villas in the best neighborhood of Asmara while disabled veterans, many paralyzed from the neck down, were forced to live in dilapidated army shacks. Ex-combatants, who were not allowed to work either in the private sector or outside their civil service status, organized a strike to protest their miserable surroundings and physical care. The president just dismissed them.

In 1993, the ex-combatants rebelled and occupied the airport, the commercial banks, and other key buildings of the capital, and then marched the president to the stadium at gunpoint. According to those who were present, the insurrectionists charged the leadership (although not the president) with blatant corruption. More importantly, they charged Isaias with abandoning the principle of collective leadership and replacing it with a one-man rule that bordered on dictatorship. Reminding him of his broken promises of demobilization and of providing financial compensation for the families of martyred combatants, they demanded to know how he planned to address the mounting social injustices. He listened to their grievances, admitted that mistakes had been made (but not by him), promised to take corrective action, and assured them that no punitive action would be taken against any members of the insurrection.

What was extraordinary about this encounter was the restraint shown by well-armed, battle-hardened ex-combatants while they were virtually in total control of the government. They could have mounted a *coup d'état* or simply shot the president, but they let him go. Not surprisingly, as soon as he was released, he promptly jailed all the leaders of the insurrection. As a token gesture, he convened a military tribunal of officers of his choice and established a "Special court"—a kangaroo court—to prosecute a few government officials for corruption. As it happened, the leaders of the insurrection were the first victims of the court, but no government official was ever brought to justice.

That same year, Isaias announced that all Eritreans would henceforth have to spend two years in national service. This would entail six months of rigorous military training in the notorious Sawa training camp—renowned for its use of harsh discipline and torture, exploitation of combatants as free labor, and brutality toward women—and eighteen months in public service. By making such national service compulsory, the government hoped to encourage a sense of unity among men and women across all the different ethnic groups and give them a stake in their country. Perhaps most important, compulsory national service would establish a cheap labor pool, reduce the country's dependence on foreign aid, and check the corruption that such aid brings with it.

Evasion of military duty was severely punished, with sentences ranging from ten years of "vigorous imprisonment" to torture or execution, depending on the circumstances. Military police and soldiers patrolled the city's main streets with Kalashnikovs at the ready, stopping all young people and demanding to see their travel papers. Those who could not produce the right documents were packed into open trucks and either shipped off directly to the front lines or first sent to the Sawa camp. To keep young people of draft age from escaping, the government required families that could not account for the whereabouts of their children to pay exorbitant fines; those who didn't have enough money were jailed. A lucrative business in human trafficking sprang up to transport those Eritreans who could pay for it to one of the safe neighboring countries. The overwhelming majority who couldn't pay were conscripted into the army to sit aimlessly in the trenches.

International human rights organizations with observers in the field, such as Amnesty International and Human Rights Watch, reported that female conscripts within a suitable age range were routinely raped or became the unwilling concubines of senior officers. Hearing such rumors, as well as those of suicide and torture, first hundreds, then thousands, and eventually tens of thousands of young people fled the country. Armed guards of the PFDJ patrolled the borders with orders to shoot on sight anyone who tried to cross them. But eventually, they, too, had enough and joined those who were fleeing the country.

Many of the young people who fled were granted political asylum in Sudan, Ethiopia, and other countries across the globe. The largest contingent of Eritrean students abroad were pursuing advanced studies in South Africa. When their visas expired, they refused to return home, and because their passports were now invalid, the South African government granted them political asylum. Safely settled in South Africa, they established a radio station that could broadcast deep into Eritrean territory to denounce the Eritrean government's ruthless and insane policies.

Not long after, when members of the disabled veterans association mounted a second protest, the president ordered the police to suppress the insurrection by force, and several of the veterans were killed while organizers were jailed by the same kangaroo court. There was no excuse for such brutality. It was simply the actions of a few people who, taking advantage of a hopeful liberated nation, hijacked it and amassed excess power and were determined to maintain it.

· 1 9 ·

ANOTHER WAR

When I returned to Asmara in 1998, the air was full of rumors that the Ethiopian army was preparing to attack Eritrea. On my third day there, the calm was shattered by an air raid alarm. Assefaw and I had just finished lunch, and I was on my way back to the Asmara Children's Home when an Ethiopian fighter jet suddenly swooped down over the city, brought all traffic to a halt, and then disappeared without firing a shot. When I asked Assefaw what was going on, he smiled enigmatically and said nothing, but he had a very good idea what this overflight meant.

As I reached the orphanage, which was next to the Asmara airport, the MIG returned and dropped a single bomb on the airport runway. Upon hearing the explosion, the director of the orphanage rushed out of his office, screaming at his staff to bring the children to safety, but there was no place to hide.

Although an aerial attack on Asmara had until now been unthinkable, the EPLA had prepared for such an eventuality by placing well-spaced antiaircraft batteries around Asmara. As soon as the MIG had unloaded its bomb, which caused relatively little damage, Eritrean antiaircraft weapons responded with a long staccato of cannon fire, and two Soviet-made Eritrean fighter jets scrambled in pursuit. When the MIG didn't return for another bombing run, everyone assumed that this had simply been a warning shot.

That evening, Assefaw came by the house where I was staying to make sure that I hadn't been hurt. As we talked about the possible meaning of one isolated bombardment, a stream of open trucks passed by filled with exuberant boys waving a parachute, yelling nonsensical patriotic slogans, and celebrating "their" victory. Apparently, the Ethiopian pilot had been shot down on his way to home base, had bailed out, and was captured without a struggle. The parachute the boys were waving was the one the pilot had used when his MIG was shot down.

This was the only time that the Ethiopian Air Force ever bombed Asmara, but the idea that such a thing was even possible shocked the people living there. Alarmed by the prospects of another all-out war, all foreign embassies and consulates ordered their nationals to leave within twenty-four hours, and each country sent a plane to pick up its consular and diplomatic personnel. The airport was in the grips of hysteria. Large crowds of Eritrean Americans were already on the tarmac waiting for an enormous U.S. Air Force cargo plane to take them home with their mountains of luggage. Most of them had come to visit relatives they hadn't seen for twenty years, had prepared for a long stay, and had brought most of their earthly possessions with them. Told that they had to leave everything behind except for one small suitcase, the old women who had probably spent their life savings to make this trip broke down in tears, sat down, and refused to let anyone pull them up to their feet; in effect, they had organized a sit-down strike. Rumors began circulating that marauding Ethiopian soldiers had already penetrated the Eritrean defenses and crossed over into Eritrean territory. A third of Asmara's population fled into the countryside, creating a whole new generation of orphans and refugee children. In response, the Eritrean Defense Forces rolled out their own collection of Soviet tanks and pointed their cannons toward the Ethiopian tanks.

Two days later, both sides called for total mobilization, and war was declared. Because national service had become obligatory for all able-bodied men and women, the Defense Ministry was able to call up a hundred thousand reserve troops within forty-eight hours after the onset of this war. All exemptions were immediately canceled, and the upper age limit for compulsory military service was raised to fifty. By January 1999, a half million soldiers were facing each other in traditional trench warfare. Once the killing started, it escalated into an insane carnage that would continue until both sides ran out of ammunition. The commanding officers, who were veterans of the independence war, were shocked by the mindless brutality on both sides. Artillery shelling was so intense that neither side dared to retrieve its wounded from where the corpses of the slain lay rotting and stinking in the heat—heat so intense that both sides had to take time out and wait until the sands cooled off in the late afternoon before they could resume killing each other. Ultimately, thousands of families on both sides had to wait two years until the war ended before they could learn whether their children had been killed or were still waiting in the trenches.

Neither side dared to publish its own casualty figures for fear that the armies would desert en masse or turn the guns on their own officers. When each side realized they could no longer keep those figures a secret, they reported that somewhere between one hundred fifty and two hundred thousand from the opposing side had been killed in action. For months on end, the whole country was in mourning; and funerals were held every day. But the presidents of both countries continued to buy more Kalashnikovs, more ammunition, and more artillery—whatever was for sale on the black market.

Eritreans of all ages were asking themselves what had been the point of this insane carnage? Who had provoked it? How could the Eritrean and Ethiopian leaders, who were cousins by blood and had grown up together, have let the situation get so out of control that a few meaningless border skirmishes could so quickly escalate into total disaster? When Eritrea's free press asked the same embarrassing questions, the president shut down all independent newspapers and jailed the reporters and publishers. That was the funeral of Eritrea's democracy.

· 2 0 ·

THE PEACETIME ECONOMY AND ITS RAMIFICATIONS

After evaluating Eritrea's human resources, material assets, and economic history, Roy Pateman, a Professor of Comparative Politics and a longtime friend of Eritrea, concluded that a private sector–led market economy would probably fail in most of the newly constructed African countries but might nevertheless succeed in Eritrea. He sounded a strong warning, however, that if such an economy did work, it would probably come at a high cost to the poorest classes of society and might significantly curtail the civil rights and democratic freedoms for which the people of Eritrea had fought for so long.[1]

Unfortunately, that prediction turned out to be on target. By the middle of 1999, the front lines had stabilized sufficiently so that commercial airlines were flying to Asmara again. President Isaias, convinced that under his directions Eritrea would become a competitive player on the world market, invited foreign investors and rich Eritreans to invest in Eritrea's business ventures on favorable terms. Loans were secured from abroad to construct the Asmara Intercontinental Hotel at an exorbitant cost of US$85 million, making it the most expensive hotel in all of East Africa at the time. For those with a generous expense account, the hotel offered all the amenities, including an indoor as well as an outdoor swimming pool, a sauna, exercise rooms, a laundry, hair-styling salons, several bars, at least three different ethnic restaurants, fresh bathroom linens twice a day, flush toilets that worked most of the time, and a fax machine in every room. Foreign businessmen, contractors, Toyota sales representatives, airline personnel, transient NGOs, and members of international development agencies regularly booked at least half the rooms. Most of the remaining rooms were reserved for UN military officers who had been quartered in Asmara after the second war and patrolled the disputed borders. When these soldiers were reassigned to other trouble spots in the world, many of the hotel rooms remained unoccupied.

In the meantime, the combatants who had already fought for years in the trenches were eagerly waiting to be released from military service, but demobilization was postponed indefinitely. The excuse given this time for not letting veterans go home to feed their families was, of course, the continuing national emergency. As a result, the combatants became increasingly confused as to who they actually were and what place they occupied in postwar society. They were no longer combatants who had volunteered to defeat the Ethiopian army and defend their country; nor were they members of the civil society who might reap some benefit from years of sacrifice and finally be allowed to take responsibility for their families. By governmental edict, the ex-combatants were not allowed to seek part-time employment in the civilian sector. Besides, all the good jobs were now reserved for the economic arm of the PJDF, the country's only permitted political party. As long as they were conscript soldiers, the ex-combatants did receive pocket money every month in lieu of a salary, but it was less than a dollar a day—not nearly enough for them to feed their starving families as inflation got steadily worse. They were left to watch as the generals in their shiny new uniforms and the ministers of the new government appropriated some of the finest villas in Asmara and sat around the bar of the Intercontinental drinking single-malt Scotch whiskey far into the night. In public festivals, displays, and parades, EPLF fighters were still celebrated as heroes, but the civilian population was tired of war and started to see them as a nuisance that stood in the way of economic progress.

Suspicious of any grassroots self-help movement, the president had outlawed all informal veterans' associations or "rap groups," further depriving the combatants of that sense of community that had played such a critical role in sustaining them during the war. In short, the ex-combatants had been robbed of their identity.

The treasury was empty, but Isaias somehow found millions to spend on weapon systems. International financial institutions and development banks, once a major source of funding for generously endowed civilian development programs, watched with dismay and eventually withdrew all financial aid except for the very successful campaigns against AIDS, tuberculosis, and malaria.

A major puzzle in the midst of this economic scarcity was the president's decision to purchase a computerized axial tomography (CAT) device, which would consume 50 percent of the annual health budget at a critical time when the leading causes of preventable death in Eritrea were malaria, tuberculosis, and measles. The rate of preventable deaths among infants was still 151 per 1,000 live births, and the leading causes of preventable childhood illnesses were still upper-respiratory tract infections, diarrheal diseases, and perinatal complications—nearly all of which could be diagnosed, treated, and sometimes even cured by simple, well-established, and affordable public health measures that required neither a medical degree nor a CAT scan. In most cases, a hand-held stethoscope and thermometer would be much more cost-effective. On the other hand, most of the serious neurological, medical, or surgical conditions whose diagnoses might, in selected cases, benefit from a CAT scan could probably be treated more economically and effectively abroad. By now, there was nearly universal consensus among public health officers that the only effective means for addressing the enormous health burdens of the general population in underdeveloped countries was a distributed system of primary health care of the kind that Assefaw had successfully launched in the EPLF base camps—one that relied on primary prevention instead of surgical treatment.

Why, then, had a government that was once committed to guaranteeing access to adequate health care for the poor as well as for the rich allocate half of the Ministry of Health's annual budget for an elaborate, electronically driven diagnostic tool that was, at best, of marginal utility, when thousands of children were still dying needlessly every year from preventable diseases? Was it the vaulting ambition of the medical profession throughout the world? Was it Isaias's personal pride?

Even ministers who were close to the president found it increasingly difficult to decipher what Isaias actually thought or planned. Did he really expect that a rich clientele from abroad would flock to Asmara for a diagnosis of their liver cirrhosis or obesity, when many of the neighboring countries already had far more sophisticated scanning devices? One rumor that made the rounds shortly after the scanner arrived, although difficult to corroborate, offered the following explanation: When Isaias became acutely ill with a near fatal case of cerebral malaria, he was flown to the most advanced tertiary care hospital available, in Tel Aviv, Israel. Upon recovery, the president insisted that Eritrea have one or more of the same remarkable machines that the Israelis had. But, as usual, it was the children who paid the price.

These ill-conceived expenditures amounted to an unfortunate regression to a two-tiered system of medical care—one for the rich, one for the poor—that would hinder support for a distributed system of primary health care, as it had in many other developing countries, without generating any of the hoped-for hard currency. They were also symptomatic of the progressive alienation between the government and the poor, whose conditions in 1960 had certainly been a major impetus for the war for independence.

Several key advisors to international development banks have argued that to promote sustainable economic development, poor, under-developed countries must give high priority to large-scale capital investments at the expense of domestic spending on the well-being of the poor so as to generate hard currency. But after seeing the stark contrasts between the slums of Asmara and the glitz of the Intercontinental Hotel, and after comparing the morbidity and mortality rates among Eritrea's children whose lives could easily have been saved at a small cost, I wondered whether international development experts and macroeconomists might have gotten it wrong.

Since there will always be a dynamic and fruitful tension between a commitment to economic development, on the one hand, and to social justice and democratic freedoms on the other, each society must make difficult choices. But as far as I could tell, this government had consistently made the wrong choices—choices that would have dire consequences for Eritrea's children.

Note

1 Pateman, *Eritrea: Even the Stones Are Burning*, 241.

Part IV
THE LEGACY OF THE ZERO SCHOOL

· 21 ·

THE ORPHANS REVISITED

Clearly, the Zero School experiment in progressive education could not be carried on at the same high level in liberated Eritrea as it had been during the war. The treasury was empty; the demands on limited human resources were not compatible with the urgent need to teach large numbers of children in overcrowded classrooms; and there was an acute and chronic shortage of trained teachers, especially those familiar with the specialized Socratic method required for integrating praxis and theory. Finally—and for reasons to which I was not privy—Beraki, who had been the inspiration for the Zero School curriculum and its implementation, was removed from the Ministry of Education and transferred to the Ministry of Information; he was later appointed ambassador to Berlin.

Nevertheless, despite the hard times that the orphans had endured during the war and the difficult transition from war to a rocky peace, the levels of academic and professional achievement that they had attained after graduating from the Zero School were quite striking. Three times as many Zero School alumni as home-reared students had qualified for admission to the University of Asmara. Believing that this surprising outcome required an explanation, Gere and I set out after the war to understand how profoundly the Zero School had influenced the social and intellectual development of the orphans of the Eritrean war.

Many of the school's alumni had either been born in one of the refugee camps or raised in the Solomuna orphanage until the age of seven, when they were old enough to enroll in the Zero School. Because they had lived and studied at the school for at least five years, Gere reasoned that they would probably be able to give us a reliable impression of how well the progressive curriculum had prepared them to cope with the vicissitudes of life after independence. After a careful search of the records of the school's graduates, Gere was able to locate sixteen women and sixteen men, aged nineteen to thirty-four, who had completed their education at the Zero School in the early 1980s. These alumni had had the longest experience of learning at the school and were probably in the best position to assess how well those years had prepared them for what was to follow.

These graduates all agreed that life at the Zero School had been very hard, especially during their first few years when many were homesick, missing their families and wanting to return home but not knowing how to get there or even whether their villages still existed. Yet most of them looked back on their years at the school as the happiest time of their lives. They had belonged to a community of teachers and students who were their friends, who encouraged them to think critically and to resist and defeat unwarranted authority. What they remembered most was that their teachers always treated them (both boys and girls) with respect, acknowledged their individuality, and interacted with them as equals who had minds of their own. Many of the alumni had kept in touch with former classmates and said that, should the opportunity ever arise, they would like to return to Sahel province to see what had become of the Zero School, which, they had been told, had been overtaken by goats.

In 2002–2003, Johanna Fleischhauer, a German psychologist and political scientist, conducted detailed interviews with a selected sample of young adults who had lived at the Zero School during the mid-eighties.[1] Her far more detailed clinical findings indicated that most of the alumni in her study showed "congruent" and well-balanced behavior, were engaged in stable social relationships, studied or worked productively, and faced the postwar difficulties of the second Ethiopian war (in 1998) with confidence. They had all been supported by their families and, with one exception, had all overcome earlier emotional difficulties. Only one was upset enough to seek professional help.

Joe, who had been in charge of all teacher training at the base camps, had kept in touch with former students, nearly all of whom considered him their friend and mentor. They, too, reported having done remarkably well since independence. Among those who were now living abroad, many had become successful engineers, computer scientists, laboratory scientists, deans of prestigious medical schools, heads of profitable business enterprises, and the like. Some had joined local community associations that met regularly to discuss events at home and organize fund raisers to help poorer Eritreans in the diaspora.

Yet there were among the alumni whom Gere had been able to locate those who considered their time at the school to be the worst years of their lives. There had never been enough food or water to go around, and much of the food they received was inedible. Most of the time they felt lonely and abandoned. They lived in chronic fear of the older boys, who beat them up, stole their personal possessions, and bullied them and, when they complained, their teachers refused to get involved or do anything to stop the bullying. They always had to resolve their personal conflicts by themselves. When they were asked whether they might one day want to return to the Zero School for a brief visit, they made it very clear that nothing was further from their minds. But when Gere reviewed the school records, he discovered that almost all of those alumni who had found life at the school intolerable had been enrolled there shortly after it first opened—that is, during its earliest and most difficult period when it was still only a temporary refuge that was badly understaffed and poorly organized, when there were no trained teachers, and when severe shortages of basic food staples and other essential supplies were quite frequent. Yet the school records showed that even these graduates had adapted remarkably well during the stormy transition from war to peace.

In fact, long-term follow-up studies of orphans who had spent their early childhoods in Solomuna and then been educated at the Zero School showed that they had all done exceptionally well. Although there were very few jobs in the private sector after the Red Sea Corporation—the commercial arm of PJDF—had appropriated all lucrative employment opportunities, twice as many Zero School alumni as public school graduates held responsible jobs *not* controlled by the corporation. Five of the thirty-two whom Gere had interviewed had completed teacher training and were now qualified as elementary school teachers; two had become air traffic controllers at the Asmara airport; one was now a certified public accountant; another was a fully trained social worker in the MLHW; and one student with a talent for graphic arts was now an artist-in-residence at the Asmara museum. The entire Eritrean Air Force consisted of Zero School alumni who were now flying the same advanced

MIGs as their seasoned Ethiopian counterparts. The flight instructors, who for some reason were Russian pilots, rated the young Eritreans as excellent pilots, albeit perhaps a little "too brave." Such an outcome reinforces the impression that, given the right social context and community support, even orphans who have spent their early, most vulnerable years in an understaffed, badly overcrowded institutional setting are not necessarily doomed or permanently damaged in some way. They, too, can survive and prosper.

Most of the Zero School alumni who could be traced back to early childhood had done remarkably well, even under very difficult conditions. That finding reopened wide-ranging questions, such as whether traumatic experiences in early life have a permanent or only a transient impact on long-term outcomes. Would the curriculum that had had a powerful effect on the orphans during the war retain an equally powerful effect on them in the early postwar years? Or is it possible that positive psychosocial influences on childhood development in wartime gradually degenerate in peacetime? This would no doubt be a sad reflection on the human condition but one that at least has to be considered.

At the same time, it is instructive to compare the Zero School alumni, who had completed their secondary school education during the war years, with the Zero School students who were in the middle of their studies when the school was closed and had to complete secondary schooling elsewhere.

One of the largest of the replacement schools was a compound of barracks in the Central Highlands on the outskirts of a town called Decemhare. The compound had been abandoned by the Ethiopian soldiers who had been garrisoned there until just before the end of the war, and it was here that the former Zero School students would live while completing their studies at the local public school. The compound included several overcrowded dormitory buildings for the students, separate facilities for counselors and staff, and a very large, empty hall that had been remodeled as a communal kitchen and dining hall. Young women who wanted privacy had to wash in the dark while the young men shared a number of communal bathrooms. The teachers taught in the traditional style. While students at the Zero School had always felt secure in their relationships with their teachers, the same egalitarian ethos that had pervaded that environment was nowhere to be found in Decemhare.

To see for ourselves how these students were faring, Gere and I visited the complex, seeking the headmaster's permission to interview the students. But the headmaster was nowhere to be found, and when we finally did locate him and were able to explain the reason for our visit, he seemed to be in despair.

Many of his students were depressed about the hopelessness of their current situation and the ambiguous role they anticipated in the postwar society. Later, I discovered that he had been so deeply ashamed of not being able to help the students or recruit the personnel he needed to run a boarding school for eight hundred students that he eventually resigned.

Because most of the Decemhare students were orphans who were in the middle of their studies at the Zero School when that school was closed, a few had lived through several bombing attacks there and thus felt a kinship with the combatants with whom they had been close. Sometimes the ex-combatants made an effort to visit the students in Decemhare. Now that the war was over, however, they either had been remobilized or were desperately seeking a place to settle and earn an income to feed their families. As a result, their visits were rare, leaving the Decemhare students to feel abandoned.

Like the former combatants, the transplanted Zero School students had lost their sense of identity. They were neither fledgling fighters nor prospective university students, nor were they civilians allowed to work in the private sector. Their isolation was made even more acute by the cultural conflict that had arisen during the war between those Eritreans living in the liberated areas and those living under the heel of the Ethiopian occupation forces. The town students treated them as if they were country bumpkins and ridiculed them for their naïve honesty and refusal to tell lies, their lack of sophistication, and their indifference to social refinements. Similarly, the adults in Decemhare considered the former Zero School students rude (they didn't say "please" or "thank you"), lacking in respect for the traditions of the previous generation, disrespectful of older people, untrustworthy, and sexually provocative. They wanted nothing do with these "ruffians from the bush."

For their part, the former Zero School students despised their Decemhare classmates for cheating on exams, lying, being disrespectful toward their teachers, and stealing food from local shopkeepers. They also wanted nothing to do with the townspeople, whom they considered to be hostile, standoffish liars. It was therefore not surprising that the students felt isolated and alone, that they no longer belonged anywhere.

Yet despite these additional hardships and the growing uncertainty of their future, their years of studying, learning, teaching, and fighting at the Zero School had left a distinct stamp on the character of these young men and women. Their Decemhare teachers reported that almost all of the former Zero School students excelled in their academic work and scored in the top of their class, being far more committed to learning and better prepared for advanced work than the students who had grown up in the security of their homes and with their parents. The ex-combatants who still came to Decemhare for an occasional visit to see how the students were faring told me several times, with obvious satisfaction, that the former Zero School students were incorruptible, honest to a fault, independent minded, self-reliant, and direct to the point of bluntness in their social transactions.

When Gere interviewed these Decemhare students about their experiences at the Zero School, they didn't hesitate in the least to respond. On the contrary, they seemed relieved that at last someone was listening to their complaints. They were eager to tell their stories, so that parents and classmates would understand what life in the field had been like.

They all agreed that life in the base camps had always been harsh and often difficult to endure, but, like those who had ultimately graduated from the Zero School, most of them looked back on their years there and agreed that the hardships—the constant danger of aerial bombardment, the loss of their parents and their villages—were far outweighed by the positive experiences. What they remembered most about those years was that their teachers had always treated them with respect and encouraged them to think for themselves rather than telling them what to do and how to do it. For many of the students, and especially for the girls, the experience of teachers and students cooperating and working together as equals was entirely new. As one student put it, when the teachers showed them how to be self-sufficient and to accomplish by cooperation what they couldn't do alone, they felt useful, sometimes even proud, because they were contributing to the liberation of their country.

Now, however, they felt as if they were no longer needed. Like the combatants, they missed the reaffirmation of a community where everyone—students, teachers, counselors, and auxiliary staff—had been a major source of support during the hard times. They looked back to the "good old days" at a critical period in their lives when life had been simpler, more honest, and more fulfilling, and when it had been *their* revolution.

Note

1 Fleischhauer, *Von Krieg betroffene Kinder*.

· 2 2 ·

LOOKING FORWARD

Has the Eritrean revolution, like so many other African liberation movements, turned out to be a failure?[1] Is the country of Eritrea worse off now than it was in 1958, when efforts to resist the imperial Ethiopian regime through peaceful means were ultimately squelched, giving rise to the ELF and the conviction that armed struggle would likely be the only way out of an impossible situation?

It must have been a bitter experience for the people of Eritrea, who had fought for thirty years to create a democratic society, to see their great achievements unravel one by one. After Isaias was elected to the presidency in 1993, he quickly laid the groundwork for their newly independent country to turn into a single-party dictatorship—in effect, a prison without exits. Regarding the state of human rights in the country, Amnesty International reports that, as of 2017,

> [t]housands continued to flee Eritrea while the authorities severely restricted the right to leave the country. Indefinite mandatory national service continued to be imposed. Restrictions on the rights to freedom of expression and of religion remained. Arbitrary detention without charge or trial continued to be the norm for thousands of prisoners of conscience. Thousands were denied the right to an adequate standard of living.[2]

And as for the country's economic conditions, the economy today is stagnant, inflation keeps rising, and staggering expenditures for the latest and most modern military weapons take food away from a starving civilian population.

Of course, those who have witnessed this disintegration might find solace in the fact that the armed struggle has not been a total loss. The war actually brought about some major social benefits that would eventually improve the quality of life for future generations. For one thing, although reunification of orphans with their extended families was extraordinarily difficult, ultimately more than forty thousand orphans and families were reunited, and most of those reunifications proved to be sustainable and successful after brief periods of minor adjustment. As for those lost children who were not reunited with their extended families, more than 150 found a haven in small group homes.

For another thing, although the plans formulated in the base camps to construct a nationwide network of primary healthcare centers repeatedly had to give way to misguided healthcare policies, which called for the hasty accumulation of very expensive high-tech machines that had no preventative or therapeutic value, many thousands of children and their parents throughout the country now have access to basic public health services, immunization campaigns, and school check-ups that had never before been available to them. Moreover, thanks to the increase in mobile health services and the distribution of primary healthcare centers throughout the rural areas, many more families now have access to clean water and protected sanitary facilities, resulting in a dramatic decrease in infant mortality, childhood diseases, and endemic or pandemic infectious diseases.

Regarding education, the versions of the national curriculum hammered together after independence unfortunately had precious little to do with Beraki's revolutionary concept of school as a place where children can learn to think critically, question claims of truth by an appeal to self-evidence, and solve problems by active experimentation instead of passive memorization. But it is nevertheless true that, for the first time in Eritrea's long history, a vast majority of children are now attending elementary schools, on a space-available basis, and actually learning to read and write.

These and other postwar achievements are impressive, but they are by no means unique in the so-called developing world. Other independence struggles and socialist revolutions in Africa, South Asia, and elsewhere have made similar and even more sustainable social gains during their early postwar years. But eventually, their leaders all defaulted on their promises of social justice, free speech, public education, an independent press, the right to public assembly, and multiparty elections, and despite major advances, most have, in effect, regressed to one-man rule and outright totalitarianism.

Having witnessed how the Eritreans fought so valiantly and for so long against the far superior forces of an external enemy and ultimately prevailed, one is left wondering how this particular victory collapsed so completely and how the Eritreans came to be so disastrously betrayed from within.

The answer to that question lies beyond the scope of this book. However, those who vigorously oppose the government today still see cause for hope that a sustainable democratic society in Eritrea may yet be attained. And that hope lies with the next generation of Eritreans, those who are now young adults.

It is, of course, the next generation—the students, former students, young social activists, and others, both in the country and in the diaspora—that has the greatest stake in the future of Eritrea. Unless they give up altogether and manage to escape and settle abroad, it will be their future—and thus their responsibility to secure. Putting the burden for bringing about a bloodless regime change on their shoulders might seem hopeless, but skeptics are advised to think back to the late 1950s, when affairs of state were under the control of Haile Selassie. When the Ethiopian emperor waged war on the Tigrinya language and Eritrean culture, it was the Eritrean high school students who were the first to mount public demonstrations of protest. It was, in fact, the students who first gave political meaning to the slogan "victory to the masses" and whose protests led the way to massive strikes throughout the country. And it was the Eritrean university students enrolled at Haile Selassie University in Addis Ababa who agitated effectively for Eritrean independence from Ethiopia and eventually formed the nucleus of combatants from the Central Highlands—those who would eventually become the effective fighting arm and leadership of the EPLF.

But that was four decades ago, when the enemy was a palpable external force. The enemy is no longer a foreign invader hammering at the door. This time it is the government itself that must be overthrown—and, if at all possible, without a bloody coup. Thus, those in the next generation who are committed to continuing the struggle for a democratic state of Eritrea, one that is not only independent but also faithful to its social and economic goals, face an even more impossible task than their parents.

The task is monumental. The barriers to its achievement seem insurmountable. Who from the next generation will have the personal commitment, the vision, the political maturity, and above all the support and consent of the general population to accept the challenge? As has been noted, multitudes of those adolescents and young adults who might have provided new leadership have left the country in droves, settling in South Africa, Europe, North America, and Australia, where they have been granted political asylum by their host countries and become part of an ever-growing diaspora. Although these émigrés are committed in principle to forcing a regime change in Eritrea, they are living in other countries, and the regime change they seek will require coordinated action from within.

As for the current leadership, it will have to give way and make room for the new generation. In the Eritrean culture, old age is revered and looked to for wisdom and advice, for temperance and restraint. But, somehow, too many of the older generation caved in and compromised the principles for which they once shed their blood. The next generation probably no longer trusts them for leadership because they are no longer reliable.

But who from the next generation will have the personal commitment, the vision, the political maturity, and, above all, the support and consent of the general population to create change when the time is right to do so? Is there now a leader who can release the country from its self-imposed lethargy and indecision, who can inspire and unite the countless factions that continue to squabble in back rooms arguing empty politics, and who can heal the wounds of factionalism that have poisoned the climate of reconciliation for much too long? And if there is, where might that leader be found?

This question inevitably leads us to try to identify what qualities such a leader would possess and what conditions might have fostered their development, especially in the midst of such an adversarial environment. And that brings us back full circle to the orphans of Eritrea, those children who overcame the trauma of their childhoods—childhoods defined by the hardships endured over the course of a thirty-year war—to emerge strong, secure, and self-possessed. What was it that enabled these children to not just survive, but to thrive?

The answer, at least partially, may lie in their unique experience of growing up in the base camps of the EPLF, where they triumphed over adversity by studying and working together with their mentors toward the shared goals of freedom, social justice, and independence. Living for years in the egalitarian environment of the Zero School, these children internalized the essential values and responsibilities of the EPLF and learned to ask critical questions rather than accepting superstitions and revealed truths. Their progressive education enabled them to discover the power of their minds to resist authority when it threatened their freedom and basic human rights. It helped them find the moral strength to persevere, prosper, and become self-reliant.

Conceivably, this same dynamic will empower the next generation to pick up the gauntlet and help restore Eritrea to an open society based on democratic principles and the rule of law. The transition from illiteracy to basic literacy, as well as the introduction of preschool education after the war, made fundamental contributions to the intellectual development and social integration of its citizens into Eritrean society. Thus prepared, the next generation of children may indeed be the hope for Eritrea's future, the rallying point for a return to democratic principles of governance and informed resistance to Isaias's oppressive authoritarianism. With the Zero School alumni in the lead, there is every reason to hope that the combatants and civilian sectors of society will be able to reconcile the differences that divide their country, put their common struggle for social justice and a truly democratic society back on track without making the same mistakes as their elders, and build a truly liberated society that might once again become the hope of Africa.

Notes

1 Meredith, *Fate of Africa*.
2 Amnesty International, *Amnesty International Report 2017/18: The State of the World's Human Rights*, "Eritrea" (London, UK, 2018), 159. https://www.amnesty.org/en/wp-content/uploads/2021/05/POL1067002018ENGLISH.pdf

BIBLIOGRAPHY

Amnesty International. *Amnesty International Report 2017/18: The State of the World's Human Rights*. London, UK: Amnesty International, 2018.

Amnesty International. "Eritrea." *Amnesty International Report 2017/18: The State of the World's Human Rights*. https://www.amnesty.org/en/wp-content/uploads/2021/05/POL1067002018ENGLISH.pdf, 2018.

Christopher, Warren. "The United States and Africa: A New Relationship." Address before the 23rd African-American Institute Conference, Reston, Va., 21 May 1993. http://dosfan.lib.uic.edu/ERC/briefing/dossec/ 1993 /9305/930521dossec.html.

Connell, Dan. *Against All Odds: A Chronicle of the Eritrean Revolution with a New Afterword on the Postwar Transition*. Lawrenceville, NJ.: Red Sea Press, 1997.

Connell, Dan, and Tom Killion. *Historical Dictionary of Eritrea*. 2nd ed. Lanham, Md.: Scarecrow Press, 2010.

Duckworth, Eleanor. *The Having of Wonderful Ideas: And Other Essays on Teaching and Learning*. 3rd ed. New York: Teachers College Press, 2006.

Ericsson, U. *A Profile of Orphanages in Eritrea*. Asmara, Eritrea: Authority of Social Affairs, Republic of Eritrea, 1985.

Firebrace, James, with Stuart Holland. *Never Kneel Down: Drought, Development and Liberation in Eritrea*. Nottingham, UK: Spokesman for War on Want, 1984.

Fleischhauer, Johanna. *Von Krieg betroffene Kinder*. Opladen, Germany, and Farmington Hills, Mich.: Budrich Uni Press, 2008.

Gottesman, Les. *To Fight and To Learn: The Praxis and Promise of Literacy in Eritrea's Independence War*. Lawrenceville, NJ.: Red Sea Press, 1998.

Halberstam, David. *The Best and the Brightest*. New York: Random House, 1972.

Jareg, Elizabeth. *Report on Consultancy Visit to Eritrea*. Oslo, Norway: Redd Barna, 1988.

Jensen, Peter S., and Jon Shaw. "Children as Victims of War: Current Knowledge and Future Research Needs." *Journal of the American Academy of Child and Adolescent Psychiatry* 32 (July 1993): 697–708.

Kaler, Sandra R., and B. J. Freeman. "Analysis of Environmental Deprivation: Cognitive and Social Development in Romanian Orphans." *Journal of Child Psychology and Psychiatry* 35.4 (1994): 769–781.

Kemey, Issayas. *Issayas' Blog*, 11 Jan. 2014. http://kemey.blogspot.com/2014/01/a-conversation-with-solomon-tsehaye_11.html.

McCall, John N. "Research on the Psychological Effects of Orphanage Care: A Critical Review." *Rethinking Orphanages for the 21st Century*. Ed. R. B. McKenzie. Thousand Oaks, CA: Sage Publications, Inc., 1999. 127–150.

McKenzie, Richard B. "Rethinking Orphanages for the 21st Century: A Search for Reform of the Nation's Child Welfare System." *Rethinking Orphanages for the 21st Century*. Ed. R. B. McKenzie. Thousand Oaks, CA: Sage Publications, Inc., 1999. 289–308.

McKenzie, Richard B., ed. *Rethinking Orphanages for the 21st Century*. Thousand Oaks, CA: Sage, 1999.

Meredith, Martin. *The Fate of Africa: A History of Fifty Years of Independence*. New York: Public Affairs, 2005.

Ministry of Labour and Human Welfare (MLHW), Republic of Eritrea. *Impact Assessment of the Orphan Reunification Project*. Asmara, Eritrea: Government of the State of Eritrea, 1998.

Montessori, Maria. *The Child, Society, and the World. Unpublished Speeches and Writings*. Ed. Gunter Schulz-Benesch and Trans. Caroline Juler, Heather Yesson. Oxford, UK: Clio Press, 1989.

Morah, E., S. Mebrathu, and K. Sebhatu. "Evaluation of the Orphans Reunification Project in Eritrea." *Evaluation and Program Planning* 21.4 (1998): 437–448.

Pateman, Roy. *Eritrea: Even the Stones Are Burning*. Rev. ed. Lawrenceville, NJ: Red Sea Press, 1998.

Piaget, Jean. *To Understand Is to Invent: The Future of Education*. Trans. George-Anne Roberts. New York: Grossman, 1973. http://unesdoc.unesco.org/images/0000/000061/006133eo.pdf.

Plaut, Martin. "Who Is Isaias Afwerki, Eritrea's Enigmatic Dictator." *Newsweek*, 1 Nov. 2016. http://www.newsweek.com/who-isaias-afwerki-eritreas-enigmatic-dictator-515761.

Pool, David. *From Guerrillas to Government: The Eritrean People's Liberation Front*. Athens, Ohio: Ohio University Press, 2001.

Selassie, Bereket Habte. *The Making of the Eritrean Constitution: The Dialectic of Process and Substance*. Lawrenceville, NJ: Red Sea Press, 2003.

Taye, Adane. *A Historical Survey of State Education in Eritrea*. Asmara, Eritrea: Educational Materials Production and Distribution Agency, Ministry of Education, Republic of Eritrea, 1991.

United Nations Children's Fund (UNICEF). *The State of the World's Children 2005: Childhood under Threat*. New York: UNICEF, 2004. https://www.unicef.org/sowc/archive/ENGLISH/The%20State%20of%20the%20World%27s%20Children%202005.pdf.

Werner, David, with Carol Thuman and Jane Maxwell. *Where There Is No Doctor: A Village Health Care Handbook*. Berkeley, CA: Hesperian Health Guides, 1977.

Wolff, Peter H., and Gebremeskel Fesseha. "The Orphans of Eritrea: A Five-Year Follow-Up Study." *Journal of Child Psychology and Psychiatry* 40.8 (1999): 1231–1237.

Wolff, Peter H., Bereket Tesfai, Habtab Egasso, and Tesfay Aradomt. "The Orphans of Eritrea: A Comparison Study." *Journal of Child Psychology and Child Psychiatry* 36.4 (1995): 633–644.

Wrong, Michela A. *I Didn't Do It for You: How the World Betrayed a Small African Nation*. New York: HarperCollins, 2005.

ADDITIONAL RESOURCES

Aboud, Frances E., Mesfin Samuel, Alem Hadera, and Abdulaziz Addus. "Intellectual, Social and Nutritional Status of Children in an Ethiopian Orphanage." *Social Science and Medicine* 33.11 (1991): 1275–1280.
Achenbach, Thomas M., and Craig Edelbrock. *Manual for the Child Behavior Checklist and Revised Child Behavior Profile*. Burlington, Vt.: University of Vermont, 1983.
Ahmad, A., and K. Mohamad. "The Socio-Emotional Development of Orphans in Orphanages and Traditional Foster Care in Iraqi Kurdistan." *Child Abuse and Neglect* 20.12 (1996): 1161–1173.
Albus, Kathleen E., and Mary Dozier. "Indiscriminate Friendliness and Terror of Strangers: Contributions from the Study of Infants in Foster Care." *Infant Mental Health Journal* 20.1 (1999): 30–41.
Anatoli (Kuznetsov), A. *Babi Yar: A Document in the Form of a Novel*. Uncensored and Expanded Version. Trans. David Floyd. New York: Farrar, Straus and Giroux, 1970 [First published in 1966 in *Yunost* as "Babi Yar."]
Anda, Robert F., Vincent J. Felliti, J. Douglas Bremner, John D. Walker, Charles Whitfield, Pruce D. Perry, Shanta R. Dube, and Wayne H.Giles. "The Enduring Effects of Abuse and Related Adverse Experiences in Childhood: A Convergence of Evidence from Neurobiology and Epidemiology." *European Archives of Psychiatry and Clinical Neurosciences* 256.3 (2006): 174–186.
Axelrod, Robert. *The Evolution of Cooperation*. New York: Basic Books, 1984.

Bowlby, John. *Maternal Care and Mental Health*. Geneva, Switzerland: World Health Organization, 1952.

———. "The Nature of the Child's Tie to His Mother." *International Journal of Psycho-Analysis* 39 (1958): 350–373.

Brown, Seyom. *The Causes and Prevention of War*. New York: St. Martin's Press, 1987.

Chisholm, Kim, Margaret C. Carter, Elinor W. Ames, and Sara J. Morison. "Attachment Security and Indiscriminately Friendly Behavior in Children Adopted from Romanian Orphanages." *Development and Psychopathology* 7.2 (1995): 283–294.

Cichetti, Dante, Sheree L. Toth, and Michael Lynch. "The Developmental Sequelae of Child Maltreatment: Implications for War-Related Trauma." *The Psychological Effects of War and Violence on Children*. Ed. Leavitt and Fox. 41–74.

Colton, M. "Dimensions of Foster and Residential Care Practice." *Journal of Child Psychology and Psychiatry* 29.5 (1988): 589–600.

Connell, Dan. *Conversations with Eritrean Political Prisoners*. Lawrenceville, NJ: Red Sea Press, 2004.

Davidson, Basil, Lionel Cliffe, and Bereket H. Selassie, eds. *Behind the War in Eritrea*. Nottingham, UK: Spokesman, 1980.

Department of Social Affairs, Republic of Eritrea. *Proposals and Recommendations to Meet the Psychological Needs of Orphans in Eritrea*. Asmara, Eritrea: Republic of Eritrea, 1991.

Dunn, Judy, and Shirley McGuire. "Sibling and Peer Relationships in Childhood." *Journal of Child Psychology and Psychiatry* 33.1 (1992): 67–105.

Freire, Paulo. *Education for Critical Consciousness*. New York and London: Continuum, 1974.

Freire, Paulo, and Donald Macedo. *Literacy: Reading the Word and the World*. Westport, Conn.: Bergin and Garvey, 1987.

Garbarino, James, and Kathleen Kostelny. "Children's Response to War: What Do We Know?" *The Psychological Effects of War and Violence on Children*. Ed. Leavitt and Fox. Hillsdale, N.J.:Lawrence Erlbaum, 1993. 23–40.

Garmezy, Norman. "Stressors of Childhood." *Stress, Coping, and Development in Children*, Ed. Garmezy and Rutter, Baltimore, MD: Johns Hopkins University Press, 1983. 113–125.

———. "Stress-Resistant Children: The Search for Protective Factors." *Recent Research in Developmental Psychopathology: Journal of Child Psychology and Psychiatry Book*, Supplement, No. 4. Ed. Stevenson. Oxford: Pergamon, 1985. 213–233.

Garmezy, Norman, and Michael Rutter, eds. *Stress, Coping, and Development in Children*. New York: McGraw-Hill, 1983.

Goldfarb, William. "Effects of Psychological Deprivation in Infancy and Subsequent Stimulation." *American Journal of Psychiatry* 102.1 (1945): 18–33.

Gruber, Alan R. *Children in Foster Care: Destitute, Neglected… Betrayed*. New York: Human Sciences Press, 1978.

Hamilton-Giachritsis, Catherine, and Kevin Browne. "Forgotten Children? An Update on Young Children in Institutions across Europe." *Early Human Development* 88.12 (2012): 911–914.

Harris, Judith Rich. "Where Is the Child's Environment? A Group Socialization Theory of Development." *Psychological Review* 102 (1995): 458–489.

Hartmann, Heinz. *Ego Psychology and the Problem of Adaptation.* Translated by David Rapaport. New York: International Universities Press, 1939.

Hodges, Jill, and Barbara Tizard. "IQ and Behavioural Adjustment of Ex-Institutional Adolescents." *Journal of Child Psychology and Psychiatry* 30.1 (1989): 53–75.

———. "Social and Family Relationships of Ex-Institutional Adolescents." *Journal of Child Psychology and Psychiatry* 30.1 (1989): 77–97.

Isiugo-Abanihe, Uche C. "Child Fosterage in West Africa." *Population and Developmental Review* 11.1 (1985): 53–73.

Johnson, Dana E. "Adoption and the Effect on Children's Development." *Early Human Development* 68.1 (2002): 39–54.

Kibreab, Gaim. *Eritrea: A Dream Deferred.* Suffolk, UK: James Currey, 2009.

Kolakowski, Leszek. *Toward a Marxist Humanism.* New York: Grove Press, 1968.

Leavitt, Lewis A., and Nathan A. Fox, eds. *The Psychological Effects of War and Violence on Children.* Hillsdale, NJ: Lawrence Erlbaum Associates, 1993.

Levine, Anthony, ed. *Orphans and Other Vulnerable Children: What Role for Social Protection?* SP Discussion Paper No. 0126. Proceedings of a World Bank/World Vision Conference, 6–7 June 2001. Washington, D.C.: World Bank, October 2001.

Levy, Zvi. "Conceptual Foundations of Developmentally Oriented Residential Education: A Holistic Framework for Group Care That Works." *Residential Education as an Option for At-Risk Youth.* Ed. Jerome Beker and Doug Magnuson. New York: Haworth Press, 1966. 69–97.

Lightfoot, David. *The Development of Language: Acquisition, Change, and Evolution.* Malden, Mass., and Oxford, UK: Blackwell, 1999.

London, Ross D. "The 1994 Orphanage Debate: A Study in the Politics of Annihilation." *Rethinking Orphanages for the 21st Century.* Ed. McKenzie. Thousand Oaks, CA: Sage Publications Inc., 1999. 79–91.

McKenzie, Richard B., ed. *Rethinking Orphanages for the 21st Century.* Thousand Oaks, CA: Sage, 1999.

Nsamenang, A. Bame. "Psychology in Sub-Saharan Africa." *Psychology and Developing Societies* 5.2 (1993): 171–184.

Papstein, R. *Eritrea: Revolution at Dusk.* Lawrenceville, NJ: Red Sea Press, 1991.

Piers, Maria, ed. *Play and Development: A Symposium with Contributions by Jean Piaget, Peter H. Wolff, Rene A. Spitz, Konrad Lorenz, Lois Barclay Murphy, Erik H. Erikson.* New York: Norton, 1972.

Powell, G. F., J. A. Brasel, and R. M. Blizzard. "Emotional Deprivation and Growth Retardation Simulating Idiopathic Hypopituitarism. I. Clinical Evaluation of the Syndrome." *New England Journal of Medicine* 276.23 (1967): 1271–1278.

Prasad, Devi. *Gandhi and Revolution.* New Dehli, India, and Oxfordshire, UK: Routledge, 2012.

Randall, Margaret. *Gathering Rage: The Failure of 20th Century Revolutions to Develop a Feminist Agenda.* New York: Monthly Review Press, 1992.

Rein, M., T. E. Nutt, and H. Weiss. "Fostering Family Care: Myth and Reality." *Children and Decent People.* Ed. Alvin L. Schorr. New York: Basic Books, 1974. 24–52.

Roy, Penny, Michael Rutter, and Andrew Pickles. "Institutional Care: Risk from Family Background or Pattern of Rearing?" *Journal of Child Psychology and Psychiatry* 41.2 (2000): 139–149.

Rutter, Michael. "Developmental Catch-Up, and Deficit, following Adoption after Severe Global Early Privation." *Journal of Child Psychology and Psychiatry* 39.4 (1998): 465–476.

———. "Resilience Reconsidered: Conceptual Considerations, Empirical Findings, and Policy Implications." *Handbook of Early Childhood Intervention*. Ed. Shonkoff and Meisels. Cambridge, UK: Cambridge University Press, 2000. 651–682.

Rutter, Michael R., Eric Taylor, and Lionel Hersov, eds., *Child and Adolescent Psychiatry: Modern Approaches*. 3rd ed. Oxford, UK: Blackwell Science, 1994.

Sen, Amartya. *Development as Freedom*. New York: Anchor Books, 1999.

Shonkoff. Jack P., and Samuel J. Meisels, eds. *Handbook of Early Childhood Intervention*. 2nd ed. Cambridge, UK: Cambridge University Press, 2000.

Spitz, Rene A. "The Role of Ecological Factors in Emotional Development." *Child Development* 20.3 (1949): 145–155.

Stevenson, J. E., ed. *Recent Research in Developmental Psychopathology*. Oxford, UK: Pergamon Press, 1984.

Tizard, Barbara, and Jill Hodges. "The Effect of Early Institutional Rearing on the Development of Eight Year Old Children." *Journal of Psychology and Psychiatry* 19.2 (1998): 99–118.

Tronvoll, Kjetil. *The Lasting Struggle for Freedom in Eritrea*. Oslo, Norway: Stromme Foundation, 2009.

United Nations. *Millennium Development Goals Report, 2010*. New York: United Nations, 2010. http://www.un.org/millenniumgoals/pdf/MDG%20Report% 202010%20En%20 r15%20-low%20res%2020100615%20-.pdf.

Werner, Emmy E., and Ruth S. Smith. *Vulnerable but Invincible: A Study of Resilient Children*. New York: McGraw-Hill, 1982.

Whetten, Kathryn, Jan Ostermann, Rachel A. Whetten, Brian W. Pence, Karen O'Donnell, Lynne Messer, Nathan M. Thielman, and the Positive Outcomes for Orphans (POFO) Research Team. "A Comparison of the Wellbeing of Orphans and Abandoned Children Ages 6–12 in Institutional and Community-Based Care Settings in 5 Less Wealthy Nations." *PLoS One* 4.12 (2009). http://journals.plos.org/plosone/article?id=10.1371/journal.pone.0008169.

Wolff, Peter H. "War and the Children of Eritrea." *Report of First Eritrean International Conference on Primary Health Care*. Milan, Italy, 1986.

Wolff, Peter H., Yemani Dawit, and Berhane Zere. "The Solomuna Orphanage: A Historical Survey." *Social Science and Medicine* 40.8 (1995): 1133–1139.

Wolins, Martin. "Group Care: Friend or Foe?" *Social Work* 14.1 (1969): 35–53.

Wolkind, Stephen, and Alan Rushton. "Residential and Foster Family Care." *Child and Adolescent Psychiatry: Modern Approaches*. Ed. Rutter, Taylor, and Hersov. Oxford, UK: Blackwell Science, 1995. 252–266.

World Health Organization (WHO). *Expert Committee on Mental Health, Report on the Second Session, 1951*. Technical Report Series #31. Geneva, Switzerland: WHO Monographs, 1951.

Wright, Margaret MacFarlane. "Who Will Mow the Lawn at Boys Town?" *Rethinking Orphanages for the 21st Century*. Ed. McKenzie. Thousand Oaks, CA: Sage Publications, Inc., 1999. 207–226.

BIOGRAPHICAL DATA

Until his retirement, Peter H. Wolff, MD, was a Professor of Psychiatry at Harvard Medical School and a Senior Associate in Psychiatry at the Children's Hospital Medical Center. His scientific career included a wide range of accomplishments. For over 60 years he has been recognized as a world-renowned authority for his innovative observational studies on the development of infant behavioral states of waking and sleep, work that influenced scholars such as Jean Piaget, Heinz Prechtl, and Berry Brazelton, among others. His investigation of the different rhythmic patterns of sucking and crying by infants led to studies of the development of motor timing control, which helped reveal the neuromotor basis of dyslexia. Dr. Wolff's concern that drug effects might vary across different ethnic groups prompted his research on the physiological basis of the alcohol flushing response in Asians. His research on the relationship between socioeconomic status (SES) and neuromotor development revealed different long-term outcomes correlated with SES. Children and adolescents with slower than average development of neuromotor control tend to experience interpersonal conflicts which drive lower SES individuals into the societal legal system, whereas their middle and high SES peers are directed to the mental health system. In addition to his research, Dr. Wolff served for 35 years as chair of Children's Hospital's Institutional Review Board

(IRB), a committee established to review clinical/medical research procedures that involve humans to ensure that they meet strict ethical guidelines.

Dr. Wolff has also dedicated decades of his life advocating for the psychological, medical, and social health of child victims of war. In the 1970's, Dr. Wolff was a member of Medical Aid for Indochina and the Committee of Responsibility, organizations dedicated to evacuating Vietnamese children who had been severely burned by napalm bombs to the US and Europe for treatment, and to sending medical equipment and supplies to Vietnam to treat victims of war. A decade later, Dr. Wolff was deeply involved in the care of orphans in war-torn Eritrea, where a generation of children was being raised in orphanages and group homes under combat conditions and with minimal resources. On his many visits to Eritrea over a 30-year span, Dr. Wolff gave recommendations to the caregivers on how to improve the social and psychological conditions for the children, offering whatever advice he could to create decent and humane social environments for thousands of war orphans. The story of these children and Dr. Wolff's observations on the effects of war and orphanage conditions on development from infancy to adulthood are the topic of this book.

Studies in Criticality

General Editor
Shirley R. Steinberg

Counterpoints publishes the most compelling and imaginative books being written in education today. Grounded on the theoretical advances in criticalism, feminism, and postmodernism in the last two decades of the twentieth century, Counterpoints engages the meaning of these innovations in various forms of educational expression. Committed to the proposition that theoretical literature should be accessible to a variety of audiences, the series insists that its authors avoid esoteric and jargonistic languages that transform educational scholarship into an elite discourse for the initiated. Scholarly work matters only to the degree it affects consciousness and practice at multiple sites. Counterpoints' editorial policy is based on these principles and the ability of scholars to break new ground, to open new conversations, to go where educators have never gone before.

For additional information about this series or for the submission of manuscripts, please contact:

> Shirley R. Steinberg, General Editor
> msgramsci@gmail.com

To order other books in this series, please contact our Customer Service Department:

> peterlang@presswarehouse.com (within the U.S.)
> orders@peterlang.com (outside the U.S.)

Or browse online by series:

> www.peterlang.com

www.ingramcontent.com/pod-product-compliance
Lightning Source LLC
Chambersburg PA
CBHW052100300426
44117CB00013B/2211